Reflections on James Joyce

Stuart Gilbert at the time that he was beginning to keep his "James Joyce Journal." HRHRC Collections.

When Stuart Gilbert and the others write discerningly, soundly, penetratingly—and they do frequently—I understand why they have fastened on Joyce. Joyce loomed up big, he is a huge morsel, his proportions seem colossal by comparison with his contemporaries—but they are only attaching themselves to him like suckers because they can feed longer—and since it is not meat they require but dead inert matter (stuff of their own stuff) he is eminently and peculiarly satisfactory as alimentation. They are not searching for men, but for ideas—the last war, the war of scholars and critics, cannibalism, when dog eats dog. I want to stand aside and watch this warfare—it amuses me.

Henry Miller

Reflections on James Joyce
Stuart Gilbert's Paris Journal

Edited by Thomas F. Staley and Randolph Lewis

*Published in cooperation with the
Harry Ransom Humanities Research Center,
University of Texas at Austin*

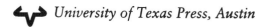 University of Texas Press, Austin

Library of Congress Cataloging-in-Publication Data
Gilbert, Stuart, 1883–1969.
  Reflections on James Joyce : Stuart Gilbert's Paris journal / edited by Thomas F. Staley and Randolph Lewis.
      p.   cm.
  "Published in cooperation with the Harry Ransom Humanities Research Center, University of Texas at Austin."
  Includes index.
  ISBN 0-292-77671-3 (alk. paper)
  1. Joyce, James, 1882–1941—Biography. 2. Joyce, James, 1882–1941—Correspondence. 3. Paris (France)—Intellectual life—20th century. 4. Novelists, Irish—20th century—Correspondence. 5. Novelists, Irish—20th century—Biography. 6. Gilbert, Stuart, 1883–1969—Diaries. I. Joyce, James, 1882–1941. II. Staley, Thomas F. III. Lewis, Randolph, date. IV. Title
PR6019.09Z53354 1993
823'.912—dc20
[B]   92-32333

Contents

Moune Gilbert, age 20. HRHRC Collections.

Acknowledgments

The editors would like to thank the following individuals for their assistance: Moune Gilbert, James Emmons, Carlton Lake, Hugh Kenner, Danis Rose, Phillip Herring, David Hayman, R. J. Schork, Clive Hart, Robin Bradford, and John Kirkpatrick. In particular, Carlton Lake's intimate knowledge of the Parisian literary scene of the 1920s and thirties and Danis Rose's expertise on Joyce's compositional techniques proved indispensable to this project; we are grateful to them both. We would also like to express our gratitude for permission given by the Society of Authors—and especially Roma Woodnutt—on behalf of the Estate of James Joyce to publish the letters of James Joyce that conclude this volume.

T.F.S.
R.L.

James Joyce, Moune Gilbert, and Stuart Gilbert, Salzburg, 1927. While on this trip Joyce proposed that Gilbert write his biography. Gilbert declined, "perhaps feeling that he would be called upon to interpret Joyce in Joyce's way rather than his own" (Ellmann 631). HRHRC Collections.

James and Nora Joyce, Salzburg, 1927 (Ellmann 631). HRHRC Collections.

Introduction

Stuart Gilbert's account of his relationship with James Joyce was discovered among the rich and voluminous papers in Gilbert's archive which was acquired by the Harry Ransom Humanities Research Center in the spring of 1989.[1] The Gilbert collection and especially Gilbert's journal give ample evidence of his extremely close collaboration on the French translation of *Ulysses*, his substantial work with the Odyssey Press (1932) and the Limited Editions Club (1935) editions of *Ulysses,* as well as his close work with Joyce on the early stages of *Finnegans Wake.* As Patrick McCarthy has noted in an essay on Gilbert's study of *Ulysses*, "It would be difficult to imagine a Joyce critic and scholar who played a greater variety of significant roles, at crucial times, than Stuart Gilbert." Besides his seminal *James Joyce's "Ulysses": A Study* (1930) and his work with Joyce during the formative stages of *Finnegans Wake,* Gilbert also contributed a succession of articles on the *Wake* and edited the first volume of Joyce's letters.

Although literary history will inevitably link Stuart Gilbert to Joyce, his major contribution to twentieth-century literature lies in his brilliant English translations of Malraux, Saint-Exupéry, Sartre, Simenon, and Camus, among the French authors. Translation, however, was a second and belated career for Gilbert. It was from Oxford, where Gilbert took a First in Classical Moderations, that he joined the Indian Civil Service in 1907, serving nearly twenty years in Burma, with a brief stint in Mesopotamia in 1918–19. Although Burma was an English colony, a version of French remained the practical language of civil administration, and there Gilbert's interest in French literature was deepened. By 1925 he was able to retire on a modest pension and to settle with his French wife, Moune, in Paris, hoping to become somehow engaged in the Paris literary world. Except for a brief period during the Second World War spent in Wales, Gilbert resided in Paris until his death in 1969. For someone with Gilbert's talents, sympathies, interests, and ambitions, Paris in 1925 was an ideal locus. Although not endowed with a creative imagination, he was brilliant at languages and could write with precision and style.

According to Moune Gilbert's account, not long after their arrival in Paris, during one of their frequent walks through the Latin Quarter, Stuart and she passed the familiar windows of Sylvia Beach's bookshop, Shakespeare and Company. On display with copies of the now-famous blue-bound volumes of *Ulysses* were several typescript pages of passages translated into French, advertising the forthcoming French translation by the poet Auguste Morel with the assistance of the critic Valery Larbaud. While in Burma, Gilbert had read and reread *Ulysses* with admiration. The classical background of the work coupled with its stunning linguistic departures appealed to him deeply. Studying the translated passages in the window, Gilbert remarked to his wife that there were several serious errors in the French rendering.

Upon entering the shop, Gilbert introduced himself to Miss Beach and commented immediately on the translation. Beach, impressed with the Englishman's observations, took his name and phone number and suggested that Joyce, who was personally involved in the translation, would no doubt contact him. The next day Joyce called Gilbert and arranged a meeting. The call was the beginning of a close and sustained literary collaboration as well as friendship that, as Gilbert remarks in his introduction to Joyce's letters, only ended with Joyce's death. As his journal makes clear, however, Gilbert's deeper feelings about the relationship were far more complex.

Characteristic of such works, Gilbert's journal is spasmodic and unsure in purpose as it relates the writer's unresolved tensions and ambivalence in his often candid and ironic observations. The journal as it exists today is not unretouched. Contained in the archive are three copies of a typescript, one with corrections, as well as the manuscript version from which the transcription in this volume was made. Although the journal contains a portrait of Joyce that is at variance with Gilbert's published descriptions, there is clear evidence to suggest that at one time Gilbert had some notion to publish the journal, probably not entertaining the idea seriously until after Nora's death. But it appears he filed the journal away and never attempted to publish it. Had he planned to publish it he would have certainly altered passages and perhaps made it a more distant, less personal recollection, but this is speculation.

The journal dates from 1 January 1929 to 26 March 1934. The journal records Gilbert's thoughts, reactions, and feelings about various people who made up Joyce's Paris circle, with whom Gilbert had frequent contact during these five years. Although Gilbert attempts to stand back and watch with cynicism and irony the dynamics of the various people surrounding Joyce, measuring their stock as it were, he reveals his own concern for his place in the circle. He knows he is of immense value to Joyce, but he is also unhappily aware that he is, both by his own disposition and circumstance, not as close or involved in the Joyce orbit as others of whom he writes. For this he is both grateful and at the same time resentful. That he admires Joyce and his achievements is evident. His cynicism, however, is more clearly revealed when he writes of those who surround the master.

Gilbert's journal is an extraordinarily privileged and decidedly personal view of a great writer—how he worked or did not work, how he dealt with people, how he treated his friends and family. Gilbert's is an unadorned account. As Stanislaus was a bitter but loyal brother, Gilbert was a bitter but loyal friend, sharing Stanislaus' distaste for Joyce's profligate ways. Gilbert's own attitudes toward Joyce reveal, like Stanislaus', more of himself than he intends. There is no mistaking the ambivalence Gilbert felt towards Joyce, whose manner, motive, and mood absorb the diarist constantly. During periods when his relationship with Joyce wanes, the journal turns more personal, more inward, to such topics as Gilbert's ennui, his health, his financial state. Yet even when Gilbert digresses and dyspeptically ruminates on the fallen state of culture and taste, the presence of Joyce haunts the journal.

The portrait of Joyce in this journal is clearly at odds with the previously published comments that Gilbert made. It is an unguarded perspective, marked by acrimony, but for this no less valuable; indeed, perhaps more so.

Works such as the Gilbert journal present vexing decisions for their editors with regard to annotation. One wishes to avoid cluttering the text and annotating the obvious, but the obvious is relative. Keeping in mind that most readers of this journal will be familiar enough with Joyce, the editors compromised occasionally by providing a context for a reference or a factual note so that the reader would not have to refer to other sources for a reminder. Gilbert often used initials or nicknames when referring to the following people: Moune Gilbert (M.), Harriet Shaw Weaver (Miss W.), Mary Colum (Mrs. C.), John Sullivan (J.S., S.), Sylvia Beach (S.B.), Adrienne Monnier (A.M.), Helen Fleischman (Mrs. F.), Caresse Crosby (Mrs. C.), Valery Larbaud (V.L.), and Victor Bérard (V.B.). These have been spelled out for clarity.

Following Gilbert's journal, there is a short and provocative commentary by Gilbert on Joyce, Herbert Gorman, and Paul Léon. Written in March 1941, this document encapsulates the central themes of Gilbert's journal in one pithy and ironic outburst. The source of this text, as well as all other documents and photographs contained herein, is the Stuart Gilbert archive at the Harry Ransom Humanities Research Center.

This volume concludes with seven previously unpublished letters from James Joyce to Stuart Gilbert. Though these letters intimate the importance of their working relationship, this fact shines more clearly in other correspondence from Joyce to Gilbert, which the Joyce Estate wishes to remain unpublished. These letters are available for study in the Stuart Gilbert archive at the Ransom Center.

Thomas F. Staley
June 16, 1992

Stuart Gilbert, James Joyce, Nora Joyce, Torquay, during the summer of 1929.
In Torquay, Joyce was helping Gilbert finish his study, James Joyce's
"Ulysses," *which was published by Faber and Faber the following year.*
HRHRC Collections.

The James Joyce Journal of Stuart Gilbert

James Joyce, Moune Gilbert, Lucia Joyce, and Stuart Gilbert,
Strasbourg, 1928. Nora Joyce's hat is partially visible over her
husband's right shoulder (Ellmann xli). HRHRC Collections.

Moune Gilbert, Nora Joyce, James Joyce, Torquay, 1929. HRHRC
Collections.

January 1, 1929

Will it be possible to keep it up? Anyhow let there be a rule—no quotations from *Ulysses*. New Year's *fête* chez Joyce last night. Three dressy—Nora, Lucia Joyce, and Mrs. "Butcher."[2] André Germain, small, bald, birdlike, recalled to Robert McAlmon a *bombe* they had made together.[3] [Eugene] Jolas enthusiastic about my reading manuscripts for *transition*, proposed that I be a contributing editor whatever that may be. Leaning against the antique sideboard he absorbed vast quantities of drink and talked of his youth. Born in America—then back to Alsace, a paternal estate, then back to America. Seems genuinely thrilled by the new literature, e.g. *Work in Progress*. Champagne made me the gift of tongues and I spoke German after a fashion. Mrs. B. heard and perhaps appreciated the compliment. Rodker said he refused to publish his own works, he hopes to be known as a French writer.[4] Seems gentle and amiable, rather languid. One Mrs. Nutting informed me that some American girl wished to ask me to a cocktail party—but not for my *beaux yeux* I fancy.[5] J.J. sang his songs—*Mr. Dooley* ("A plague on both your houses")[6] and the long Irish one. All his songs are long. Afterwards he did a hornpipe with McAlmon. Adrienne Monnier, roasting in a fireside corner, seemed bored. Salon not literary enough. The weaving sister explained at length to me her work: nothing remembered.[7] Home at about 3:00 A.M. The usual *lendemain*, late and weary. A. aggrieved at comparative drabness of her *toilette:* pointed out that none of the guests were "dressy."[8] Damn Mrs. B. and her dollars. Quiet day. Revised a few proofs and read Bérard.[9]

January 4, 1929

No good regretting good resolutions unfulfilled. . . . Uneventful anyhow. [Today was] distinguished by a purchase of a second volume of *Les Phéniciens* which I had never hoped to discover. The de Velnas for tea: myself at 6:00 to J.J. then to encounter Mr. (and Mrs.) Bradley, an American literary agent.[10] But, as usual, I did the wrong thing and talked with Mrs. Joyce instead of cultivating the commercial *littérateur*. Presented another notebook to J.J.[11]

January 5, 1929

Comédie des Champs Elysées. A play "Victor," matinee.[12] Amusing but as usual humour depends too much on *un cocu,* to which is added *une pétomane*. Even the avant-garde seem unable to escape these crude commonplaces of French humour. Met Ford Madox Ford who invited me to his Thursday afternoons. If only this could lead to work.

January 6, 1929

Sunday. Work. Translation of article for ? review. Commentary.

January 13, 1929

A week of omission. Incidents—a visit to Ford. His story of James Joyce and Proust. The two lions at a dinner party. Looked at each other in silence. Proust: "As I said in my *Du côté* . . . I suppose you have read it?" J.J.: "No." Presently J.J.: "As Mr. Bloom said—I suppose you know *Ulysses*?" "No." They were silent. Then J.J. began to talk about some internal pain he had. Mr. Proust was interested at once and they talked till dawn.[13]

January 24, 1929

It is no use. One can't keep it up. An uneventful week, anyhow. Moment of greatest pleasure Schmitt's *Salomé* at the Opera with an admirable dancer Spessivtzewa [*sic*].[14] The unfortunate Mrs. Joyce needs another operation.[15] Visited J.J. three days running to finish proofs of his installment for *transition*.[16] Mrs. Fleischman did the greater part—she is an admirable secretary to Joyce. Jolas says no more of his idea to make me a "contributing editor" to *transition*. *In vino mendacitas*.[17] J.J. repeated the story of Ezra Pound's postcard to Arnold Bennett who had favorably reviewed *Ulysses*—"You have heard your Master's Voice." That was after dinner—Moune and I had gone round.

February 3, 1929

Since then, illness. A letter from Curtius approving the Hades episode.[18] Nearly complete lethargy. A little reading, much deplorable rumbling internally. *Insuffisance du foie*; I must go to Stras*burg*—*oui, monsieur, -burg*. The typical French humourist exploits mutilation (*culs-de-jatte*), disappointed love (*cocuage*), flatulence (*pétomanie*). What is funny in these things? One day I must write a *conte* with a hero *cul-de-jatte*, *pétomane et cocu*. Some joke could be worked in about "cornes." *À étudier.*

February 16, 1929

This seems to be fortnightly like the review isn't. The effects of my malaise prevent frequent *sorties*. Three visits to hospital, where Mrs. Joyce recovers from panhysterectomy; Joyce is grumpy, seems unwilling to help with *Ulysses*.[19] A spoilt god. Still, without such pride, he could hardly have carried *Ulysses* through. Monnier demands an article for the *Nouvelle Revue Française et plus vite que ça*. All very well, but I am comatose. And, being so slow, I fear to give away too much and set some speedier worker on my tracks. Jolas came to dinner on Friday. An idealist for the smashing of language. Evidently does not care for my Far East as he asks me for a contribution for the next number of *transition*. It is nearly a waste of time writing these literary reviews. *Réclame?* I wonder. *Ulysses must* be finished. But I prefer loafing and my style is crabbed as a *transition* writer's. They all suffer from jealousy of the fluent like MacCarthy and Huddleston.[20] Hence their malice. They can't express themselves so as to be understood, get tied up in knots; sound and fury.

March 5, 1929

The miser and the bookworm are the only truly happy: they can eat their cake and have it. The translation is out—a monster. The one volume obsession of James Joyce, Adrienne Monnier and company was idiotic.[21] In keeping, in fact. The Fleischman grows yet friend-

lier: probably hoping an affectionate entourage will
rivet her to her youth more fool-proofly. *Resurgam.*

Delivered to Charybdis an article *L'Ulysse de J.J.* for
the *N.R.F.*[22] Not eulogistic enough for her taste, I
think. These literary people dog-like are always either
licking each others' bodies, or else scrapping. J.J.,
urged by Giorgio, tells Scylla that the offer of $1000
for a fragment of *Work in Progress* made by an
obscure Yank, Crosby, is not enough.[23] If Picasso is
getting $500 for three or four hours work, why should
he get so little for forty or fifty? He has presented his
doctors with "vélin" copies of *Ulysses.* Giorgio pro-
tests. Mentioned this to Charybdis who delivered a
homily on the uses of generosity. (Their stock-in-trade.
All parasites laud the purveyor of *pourboires*—Librar-
ians, *Maîtres d'hôtel*, pimps, Fargues.[24]) The test seems
to be intellectual (or sensual) as opposed to material
values. One cannot say precisely why one poem or one
prostitute is better than another. Charybdis's thesis is
that your bread returns after many days. Perhaps.
But—

March 15, 1929

In the course of a drive with J.J. he expatiated on the
distaste Irish or English crowds inspire, as opposed to
the continental. Coming from a race meeting—a
menace of storm caused him to leave early—as soon as
he engaged a car, three men came rapidly from the
course and asked to be allowed to travel with him. He
was alarmed; but the men did nothing. He is clearly
proud of Phoenix Park, the largest, he says, in the
world, except the Yellowstone. Miss Weaver is still

here and I have to read bits of my commentary to her.
An analogy between the ends of *A.L.P.* and Nausicaa
which I have discovered is, it appears, being used by
Connolly in his *Life and Letters* article.[25] I am pretty
sure I read my Nausicaa episode to J.J. months ago—
though he said he had not heard it and I read it again
last week. Perhaps he is ashamed of having given my
"tip" to Connolly! After all, why should he not exploit
me?

Adrienne after promising me to come to dinner today
(whither we have invited Adrien[26] to meet her) caused
Sylvia Beach to phone yesterday to say she could not
come: a rigmaroling excuse about a concert. No doubt
some *cher maître* or South American millionaire turned
up and invited her, and Sylvia Beach is hypnotized. An
excellent business-woman, the fat one (Adrienne
Monnier). I hate this *demi-monde* of "letters"; the
marchand de mots is worse than the *marchand
d'épices*, for he expects flattery as well as cash. The
popular writer is probably less obnoxious: he sells
honest stuff—a story. But who am I to talk? Up to the
neck in their muddy intrigues. *Misère de moi!*

April 10, 1929

Reflection inspired by the maid's black stockings. The
custom of mourning ensures that for at least one brief
period of her life a woman's clothes suit her. Widow-
hood—the most charming state.

The shliterary life. The parasite is growing, not fat, but
visible to the nude eye. Article in the *N.R.F.*, castrated
and panhysterectomised, and a little buttonhole for the

good boy presented under the head "Vulgarisation," in the *N.L.*, by Meomandre [*sic*].[27]

The only interesting *rencontre* a Mrs. Sheldon (?), runner of the English players, who wants or pretends to want me to arrange a Sudermann play for them.[28] Her intention is to use me for higher things, a stepping stone, to get her clutches on the Joyces. I suppose I should feel flattered.

I am fulfilling my vocation as a typist by copying Joyce's fragment for the Crosby people.[29] Last night dinner chez Joyce—*en famille*, plus young Fernandez— a dark little Jew with a large car.[30] Unaided, I defended modern music and lapidated their god Mozart. Joyce, subtler than the others, suggested that Mozart's merit is in what he left out. But I don't think he left out anything intentionally; he put in all he knew—which wasn't much. These people want melody—that's the truth of it. Jazz has done little to inspire their perceptions—it has taught them a little rhythm, that's all. Robots, all of them.

May 9, 1929

Disgusting as the public parts of a whore. One is caught in a vicious circle. Always things to do, damned people to see. A genuine desire to stay at home and work—but continuity is impossible. *Domi mulieris vox, for[is] vox populi.* Noises. Still, in the last two days, have done Aeolus and the Wanderers and begin Scylla today.[31] Impossible to get aid, first or last, from J.J. who is still—has been for a month—absorbed in preparing, complicating the book of extracts for the

Crosby press.[32] Last month a visit from Mel; I suspect his old belief that I am "good at heart" is wavering.[33] When a "pose" lasts 20 years, really! He has still his penchant for the right thing and the "sporting life" (thank goodness he does not confuse "sport" with personal effort as they do over here). He tires easily—I suppose in a year or two I, too. The Russian Ballet is coming—I attend by force of habit only. All these capering bitches! The music is all. But our young dummies try to be cynical in music and Igor goes on lamentably trying to squeeze drops out of an orange squeezed dry. Half of profitable literature is the cultivation of "relations"—that is the hardest part, Martha's. Mary had the good time. Instigated by Joyce, [I] have sent article on *Ulysses* to *Fortnightly*. Can't conceive why they should accept it.[34] And Eugene the word-killer wishes me to sign a manifesto, praising the New Word! Why don't they learn the old ones first?[35]

May 24, 1929

From May 16th to 22nd at Monfort l'Amoury. The incursion of the Adnet *ménage* effectively destroyed my calm.[36] Extraordinary the stupidity of the woman and the vulgar noisiness of the men. The foreigner is apt to picture the French as the cultured race *par excellence,* as contrasted with the Germanic. *Je me demande.* . . . Little work done there. My brain is mud. *transition* claimed a "Thesaurus" from me of Joyce words.[37] At Joyce's behest [I] used upon them second half of my Beach article with a little preface which must have pleased Jolas. Returned, found *Fortnightly* will take my Hades, if reduced. Why? I wonder. Heaven knows what its readers will think of it; it's not even well written. Thoughts of the week. Once women wept over

unfaithful husbands; now they rejoice. The infidelity of
the husband is the liberty/opulence of the wife.[38] (How
about a parting letter: Dear Miss— I am sending you
my balls as I have no further use for them now that our
pleasant afternoons are ended. . . . [Tennis balls, of
course.])

Ballet yesterday; "Fils Prodigue" is a compromise
between "Pas d'Acier" and neo-Stravinsky. The latter
element displeases me. Dancing good—if a little too
acrobatic. It's sad to find my interest in the ballet
languishes. I suppose that any sort of "intellectual"
work—even if, like mine, mere parasitism, is, in its
way, exhausting. I see why writers and composers have
no time for such *nugas*.[39]

May 27, 1929

Since perversion is in fashion—why not tickle the
reader by leaving the sex of the second person in a
triangle indeterminate? "A" male, "B" ?, "C" female.
But what good is writing semi-pornography?
"Pashon's" [*sic*] the thing—yet I cannot even write the
word respectfully. Respect—the supreme stimulus.
Unless one's scorn is so fierce that *facit indignatio* etc.
But to despise one must have a standard. *Quo vadis?*
"We don't know where we're going but we're on the
way."

June 1, 1929

Reflections on the Socialist victory in England. The
workers will have more to eat but less pleasure in it.
They will create the decor but dirty it with their mud
and spittle. They will lose their manners for, despising
the heathen aristocrats, they will assert themselves

11

bloodily and take politeness for the mark of weakness. And they may bust the pound. If only that ape Darwin had kept his mouth shut. The fundamentalists were fundamentally right; the know-alls fundamentally inane.

August 20, 1929

Let's put down a few *souvenirs de voyage*—heaven knows why I write this in French, disgusting mannerism. First part—the stay with Mel: flat and unprofitable—tags again—his restlessness tires me. He knows not the pleasure of abstaining, cancelling an expedition, settling down to a book. The Aldershot tattoo, however, was worth the journey: a Russian ballet which, by its colossality, genuinely thrilled at times.[40] Heard community singing for the first time; a lugubrious business—as in traffic, the slowest sets the pace—and a disappointing substitute for the rhythmic sea-noise of the crowd. In a crowd of 10,000 people—the usual small vocabulary—every second there must be 10 or more people saying exactly the same words. Anyhow talk goes in bursts. Probably when one lifts his voice the others follow.

Next, Oxford. City of regrets, yet faithful in her way. No city is too old, apparently, for violation. Leaving is the one thing that can't be hurried. One gets knowledge slowly or not at all. Can't speed up digestion. Crammed foul [*sic*] digests little. Should like to live and die there. Greed, acquisitiveness far away. If one could start again—with a clean mind, good teeth, fresh palate and innards! Lucky Faust.

Torquay. The great Man to write about.[41] His wife enchanted with everything at the Imperial. Nice people, nice food, nice town! Why? Expensive dowdiness, the inferiority feeling absent amongst morons who cannot sparkle. Her own folk. The Great Man interested as usual in himself only. Pleased to have two secretaries, Mrs. Fleischman and me.

The wall-vaulting episode. Drop miscalculated. Bruised nose, knees; sprained arms. Leap in the dark. Height of drop increased in reports from 7 or 8 feet till 20 feet. The final, authorized version. Mrs. [Joyce] wanted to go to Ireland; he fears. They are enemies and treacherous. Physical danger.

Went with him to a concert of inferior troupe on pier; he was really amused by the funny old man's jests. Also to *Yellow Streak* at Theatre. Joyce thought the theme was the upsetting effects of accident, fate always throwing a spanner into the works. I pointed out that it was a problem play: can a good wife, for merely sporting reasons, adulterate? Answer, yes. Play likely to please women. Went through "Ondt" with him. *The Spectator's* criticism.[42] Mrs. S. said it was "sarcastic."[43] I modified to "ironic but friendly"; Joyce accepts my view, repeats my formula in a letter to Miss Weaver. Concocted a letter of protest—to be sent by a country clergyman—linking Joyce and Bridges (his suggestion for new letters to be added to alphabet in order to preserve vowel sounds).[44] The clergyman suggests that between the revolutionary Shem of Paris and the Shaun of England the language is in danger and we need a Society for the Preservation of Poor English. Sent letter to Miss Weaver asking her to find a suitable sender. (She failed). Joyce collects girl's papers, *Poppy's Paper*, *Peg's Journal* etc.[45] Has a wild idea of getting *A.L.P.* published in one complete number of one of these. Impossible, I think, but one never knows. Joyce observes that (1) the heroine is fair, villainess dark, (2) few references to food, except dainty things, chocs., etc., (3) on great occasions the girl wears a special dress or hat—she has only one good one. He sees that this differs from Nausicaa. . . . After Cape's refusal, have sent my manuscript to Eliot, who wants to publish *A.L.P.* in cheap edition.[46] I wonder if this, my magnum opus, is really wanted.

December 8, 1929

All these brutes and bitches think that because one is reasonable, *serviable* and, after all, why this snobbish fear of the word gentlemen?, they can exploit one for ever and ever. The proletariat, God damn them, continue their game of blackmail, whine, swindle, threaten, and the gutless loons who believe they are their masters sentimentalise and soft soap them. Oh for a *grand soir* when some of the polite worms will turn and no longer let themselves be bled (can worms bleed?) by the so-called worker, hashed up to make a horny handed holiday. Up the bourgeois and at 'em!

December 29, 1929

Yesterday the second half of my typescript left for London. The question is—what next? Have I anything to say? Yes, but it is not what "they" want. Not even neo-catholicism. Older than that: a weak and contrite heart. Moune has taught me that. If I believed (I wish I could) I'd think that they were watching over our *ménage*. . . . Humility—yet how can one be humble toward these swine and bitches, mad rationalists, with less brains than a simple fisherman, senseless, born

noseless, eyeless, earless. Phallus and cunt—that is all
they are; their bodies are like lumbering bears led by
Mr. P and/or Miss C.

J.J. is now all Sullivan. John Sullivan my John, the
"dramatic tenor" at the opera. What wirepulling! At
my last visit we (I and Giorgio) together listed the high
notes sung by Sullivan in *William Tell:* 2 C#, 15 C, etc.
This information I will give to his correspondent
friends. He is clever; such statistics will appeal to them.
He does no other work apparently—has done none for
a month, than to boost Sullivan in whom he sees what
he would like to have been. Each new arrival at the
house has to hear the story of the mistreatment of
Sullivan at great length, in English or French: how
McCormack's agent in America prevented him from
having a concert-hall, how the rest of the company in
England (Italians) sang in such a way as to spoil
Sullivan's part, how Toscanini let him down.[47] So far
Joyce has got a commending article in the *Morning
Post*.[48] He is so persistent that he should succeed. After
all, the difference between one howler and another is a
question of *réclame*. Sullivan complains of the opera
orchestra. (Of course. An opera is, I suppose, a struggle
between the vanity of the singers and the musical
conscience of the *chef d'orchestre*). I wish I'd not so
much writing on hand—or, rather, that I could place
some paying articles somewhere. But what I have to
say—merely eternal commentaries on J.J.? Joyce's only
interest in his own work has been the letter from Sir
Edmund Gosse which was shown at an exhibition of
the *Revue des Deux Mondes*, telling the editor (it was
in 1924) not to speak of Joyce who is a "charlatan"
etc.[49] Jolas wanted to publish this in *transition*—I have,

I hope, deterred him. Curious, his silly pugnacity—or, rather, I suppose it is clever journalism. . . . For such people the institution of dueling was made—to keep them in order. The absurd vanity of the French, too, duels were excellent for that. The ideas that they should be treated with respect, never "bousculés"—"Monsieur, vous êtes un sale individu." Damn their silly "rights." What they want is a good punch on the head. Humility, again! For the want of that wars [are] made, love is broken, homes destroyed. Silly women like Mrs. Fleischman cannot understand why Mr. Schwartz (the bearded image of J.C.) persists in coming after Mrs. Joyce has been rude and snubbed him.[50] *Il s'en fiche*, or, rather, he has an end to gain and has tenacity. These silly women will let themselves be turned off their course by the least bump in their way. That is why they have to depend on men. Of course this sensitiveness is the sign of the newly emancipated, the *nouveaux riches;* reacting from it, some of them become hard-boiled. But perhaps they will settle down. Anyhow, what is the future to me? When someone is killing you, it is no consolation to know that afterwards he will regret and see that he has made a huge mistake.

January 2, 1930

On New Year's eve at 10:00 a party at J.J.'s. Present: Pat and Mary Colum, Mr. and Mrs. Huddleston, my seminamesake ex-Factorovitch etc.[51] Alcoholic reconciliation between Jolas and Huddleston, despite the offensive article in a back *transition*. At 2:30, Joyce [was] very gay and dancing a jig to "Auld Lang Syne"; Mrs. Joyce, indignant, compels all to leave. She thinks he is "making a fool of himself"—but I disagree; he is a nimble dancer. If Joyce had not been a writer he'd a been a meistersinger; if not a singer, a ballerino.

Visited Monnier that afternoon. At the showing of a propaganda film at the Russian Embassy, Factorovitch, dear Stuart, sees Gide talking to Adrienne Monnier and Sylvia Beach and whispers a plea for introduction. Introduced, he tells his *cher maître* that he is a great friend of Joyce and to prove his point quotes André Gide's *dédicace* in *l'Ecole des Femmes* verbatim. Monnier explains that, as Joyce's sight is bad, Factorovich does some reading for him. Still Factorovich should succeed—he is a well-trained pleaser and takes trouble. I wonder why he left his job with Titus, however.[52] Probably he promised to get Joyce to contribute and failed, therefore ejected.

Last night surprise visit from the doctor. Curious story of a mother (in the *banlieue*) who visited the doctor with daughter aged 18; anxious because the girl had no monthlies. Examined, the girl proved to be a boy— with attenuated male organs. Mother upset brought her young sister—the same thing. *Quelle catastrophe!* They had to leave the *pays* and recommence life elsewhere. These sisters, or brothers, must be rather attractive, I imagine. Sex excites, but embitters. Without it these boygirls must be serene, fragile, yielding.

January 29, 1930
History self-repeating—again ten days' reclusion from active life and diet. Interviews with Jolas, who is restless as ever. He gets more and more antipathetic to a memorial for Harry Crosby in his next *transition* [for two] reasons: (a) that he can't forgive Crosby for

lending money and getting onto the staff; (b) probably Crosby's murder-cum-suicide has shocked Maria's family and they are letting her know what they think of *transition* and all its works. As I want to keep in touch with Mrs. Crosby, who has many merits, I shall stick out for some sort of "hommage à" Crosby. Yet I doubt if her respect for his memory will last long. At lunch she informed me that his first idea of writing poetry came from her; at Deauville he saw her writing a sonnet, enquired how it was done, was interested and said "I could do that myself," sent for books on sonnets and discovered she had told him wrong! The making of a poet. And now, too, she is prepared to admit that a poem by him in the new review *Pagany* is not up to much. She will (they say) probably consolidate her liaison with one Armand de La Rochefoucauld. *Sic transit.* But easy to understand. The manner of Harry Crosby's death was literally a "mortal offence" to her.[53]

Sample page proofs of my commentary have come in. The text is too jammed up—for economy's sake. I don't blame them: the book will probably fall flat and they will lose.

J.J. still absorbed in Sullivan; he has got in touch with Lady Cunard, said to be the mistress of Beecham, and she may get his hero launched. His interest in *Work in Progress* seems quite dormant, if not dead. His only activity is the frequentation—giving and receiving meals—of people, journalists, editors, etc., who may help his idol onto the desired pedestal. Met James Stephens at Joyce's, a little man, a leprechaun, bald with two tufts of black hair like elephant's ears on each side of his white skull, very talkative and gently paradoxical. One afternoon Joyce described a domestic battle—about Lucia's eyes and scar: the woman in tears (she is going to have her eyes straightened); walking with me, Joyce became quite human and complained of his daughter not being "normal," and her incapacity to stick to anything! Joyce in quest of normality in his family is comic. . . . Jolas says he is like the wire-pulling, intriguing politicians in America. His stunt now is to represent all the singers at the opera as being very old—Huberty he says is nearly 60, whereas he is under 40! The reason is that he hopes to make Sullivan (who is 49) look younger by contrast. Now he is going to have a group photo taken for publication—himself, Stephens and Sullivan.

Miss Weaver did him a bad turn when she gave him all that money; he can follow caprice instead of sticking to his work.

January 31, 1930

Yesterday first outing for 10 days. Duty visit to Monnier who talked gleefully and in detail of a marvellous, juicy, saucy dinner she had eaten chez some friends; she now allows occasional escapades from her regime. She thinks the Sullivan campaign of Joyce's is partly *pour se distraire*, but also because it is a disinterested way of keeping himself in the limelight and he realizes that the difficulties of putting *Work in Progress* across will never [be] overcome unless he cultivates his publicity.

After Monnier, a visit to Mrs. Crosby. We sorted out Proust proofs first.[54] Her programme of printing for the year—mostly old works—*inter alia* an "Alice" illustrated by Laurencin.[55] Harry Crosby, it seems, sent his diary (8 years of it) to Cape before his death, wishing to have it published. Cape offers 15% royalty. As it was Harry's wish to publish she is clearly "justified"—but how much is attraction to the 15% and how much duty to deceased wishes. His parents are against it. Naturally. They dislike allusions to opium for instance. These, Mrs. Crosby says are exaggerated; he really used it very little. Pose and *snobisme*—for publication. She wants, later on, to bring out a *de luxe* edition. The idea is that she "cuts" considerably the diary 1922–8 and holds back 1929 altogether. She will publish, herself, without "cuts" later. Clever.[56]

Today, chez J.J. The Sullivan campaign works well. It seems he will sing in "Tell" in London and also at a big concert in Dublin. I think J.J. has succeeded in lauching him—but time will show. Lucia appears with a bandage on her eyes; her squint was "corrected" on Wednesday.[57] A trying time wondering how her sight will be when the bandage is off.

At last J.J. has recommenced work on *Work in Progress*. The *de luxe* edition by ? soon to come out—about the old lady A.L.P., I think. Another about the City (H.C.E. building Dublin).[58] Five volumes of the *Encyclopedia Britannica* on his sofa. He has made a list of 30 towns, New York, Vienna, Budapest, and Mrs. [Helen] Fleischman has read out the articles on some of these. I "finish" Vienna and read Christiania and Bucharest.[59] Whenever I come to a name (of a street, suburb, park, etc.) I pause. Joyce thinks. If he can Anglicise the word, i.e. make a pun on it, Mrs. F.

records the name or its deformation in the notebook.[60] Thus "Slotspark" (I think) at Christiania becomes Sluts' park. He collects all queer names in this way and will soon have a notebook full of them. The system seems bad for (1) there is little hope of the reader knowing these names—most seem new even to Joyce himself, and certainly are to me. And supposing the reader, knowing the fragment dealt with *towns*, took the trouble to look up the Encyclopedia, would he hit on the 30 Joyce has selected. (2) The insertion of these puns is bound to lead the reader away from the basic text, to create divagations and the work is hard enough anyhow! The good method would be to write out a page of plain English and then rejuvenate dull words by injection of new (and appropriate) meaning. What he is doing is too easy to do and too hard to understand (for the reader). I think I shall try my hand at the simple method myself. Too much sound and fury makes unsound and furtive . . . or fudgy. He is curled on his sofa, while I struggle with Danish or Rumanian names, pondering puns. With foreign words it's too easy. The provincial Dubliner. Foreign is funny.

February 8, 1930

On Tuesday evening last amusing reunion after dinner at the *appartement meublé* occupied by the Colums. Joyce, after declining to come, changed his mind when he heard that the Irish minister, Count O'Kelly, would be there.[61] Joyce already there when we arrived. The Count arrived late and took no notice of Joyce! Joyce very silent and bored-looking, waiting for an opportunity to *débiter* his usual *rengaine* about Sullivan. No luck! O'Kelly gave him no opening and he soon left in disgust. At the end of the party Mrs. Colum begged

"At last J.J. has recommenced work on W. in P." Gilbert's journal entry for January 31, 1930. HRHRC Collections.

O'Kelly to go to the Opera. But—so far—nothing has come of it. Either O'Kelly is bored by opera (more power to him!) or doesn't approve of Joyce.

On Friday enter Miss Beach and a Mr. Kahane (who, with a Frenchman [Babou] runs a press *de luxe* here) to sign a contract for another fragment (the City) from *Work in Progress*. Joyce says he is getting 25,000 francs. Good business—for him![62] Instead of working, he spent the afternoon in converse with a Mrs. Dempsey, wife of the previous Irish minister, on

"The insertion of these puns is bound to lead him away from the basic text..." Gilbert's journal entry for February 8, 1930. HRHRC Collections.

the usual subject. A letter just appeared in a N.Y. paper accuses the tenor Volpi of "cutting" *William Tell*,[63] and repeats Joyce's story of Sullivan being prevented from singing at Chicago by McCormack's agent. The fat is in the fire. I foresee libel actions or an apology from the paper: in either case a good advertisement for Sullivan. I have too much to do: 1. Supervising translation of my "Proteus" for *Echanges*; 2. Three articles— Crosby, Jolas and Bridges—for *transition*; 3. Schwab's "film sonore"; 4. Any day now, my own proofs; 5. Black Sun work.[64]

Moune, alas, laid up with bronchitis and I'd like to stay at home with her—but I am dragged in many directions. Looking forward to the summer and freedom.

February 23, 1930

How I detest people who talk at concerts. That is why I dislike singers—for that is exactly what they do. But the vulgar crowd—*odi odi odi et arceo* (wish I could) want their music explained. They will like (the swine, the apes—but why insult animals?) the talkies for that reason. A country where there is no aristocracy left—in what country is there any left?—and there is no longer any example of decent conduct or aesthetic taste, sinks rapidly back to the savage state and demands (and gets) toys which would appeal to savages. This is inspired by the conduct of a family at a concert last night. The doctor chattered all the time and his sister (whom I had warned of my madness, as it seems to them) joined in the conversation, inspired by the presence at the Salle Gaveau—though, thank goodness, not in contiguous seats—of the little band of French humorists, Souget, Jacob, etc., with a stupid-looking Russ (Nabokof), composer of that boring ballet "Ode."[65] Worst of all Moune seems to defend these talkers and triflers. Why? Perversity, or rather a reaction against the literary swine: though, as a matter of fact, no literary bloke has shown to her the same rudeness as the Copperie woman to me, in talking through the music after I had made my "mania" clear to her.[66]

February 26, 1930

Two wasted days at the talkie studio "Tolis" at Epinay. "The cabaret of the *coeur pendu.*" Films de

Kervin (poor girl) and Schwab.[67] Persuaded Giorgio
Joyce to figure in it. First day left Paris 8:30 with him,
arrived at studio at 9:00. Nothing ready; *décor*—a little
stage, gray walls and hanging hearts everywhere. Walls
not painted but powdered. Everything everywhere
made of wood so as to burn well at the appointed time.
Lamps all shapes and sizes: in sets of threes (rectangu-
lar) hanging on pulleys from the roof; on tripods—
everything in a studio is three-footed—and the biggest
ones, like searchlights, to be clamped to the top of the
property walls (each time, cries to the workmen aloft
"be careful, see it is tight" and the poor actors under-
neath look up in terror of extinction); the biggest of all
is a *soleil plafonnier*, circular, used for group scenes.

The band (5 persons) incompetent as ever: a lot of
louts (=proletarians). Typically, the saxophonist
amused himself by putting cigarettes, lighted, to burn
on the new black *pleyel* we were using. (The Russians
with their Krauts were model rulers, I think.) From 9–
12 first day (Monday), period of waiting for the newly-
varnished floor to dry—the first delay of hundreds.
Then rehearsal with the dancers (Hegoboro & part-
ner)—all day till 6 o'clock—when the band insisted in
leaving—and I can hardly blame them. The heat of the
lamp is as bad as the glare. Throughout the day, long
breakdowns of the camera. The camera and all the
"sound" people—German, the operator (a stupid man,
I think) French. At almost every attempt some disaster
happened, the film broke or jammed or the sound
failed. Typically, after recording [dances?] before noon,
they discovered they were not using a microphone
suitable for Hegoboro's voice and all had to be done
over again. Everyone's nerves on edge. Hegoboro very

patient on the whole (I do not think she can be French); she looked 10 years older at the end of the day. Orchestra people played abominably—their "chef" always pretends he is right. In reality he is curiously incompetent, and muddles up the scores he writes by too many "fioritura"; also is obviously not sure of his harmonies and gets his accompaniment wrong in places, trying to work on the 2 usual chords all the time (and, even so, making mistakes). Self-taught, I should say. And his musicians play very roughly. On the second day—collection of all the queen birds from Montparnasse: an Indian, Japs [sic], Russians, etc. Many delays. They were finished at about 7:30. After dinner Baglia's dance. He is good, and an amiable nigger [sic]. The band, as usual, on strike and, no doubt, blackmailing Schwab for more money. The "figurants" left in a body (though some of them were needed) at 7:30. Difficult to blame them— the glare and heat wore them out.

April 28, 1930

Two months. The obstetrics of my futile book. Owing to various muddles, it will come out late. At the beginning of the month J.J. went first to Zurich then to Wiesbaden to "see" oculists. (Not back yet, I think). The addresses were given him by unknown female admirers who wrote him.[68] His Sullivan campaign has made him news and the papers were talking about "Distinguished author going blind." For the latest fragment, "Haveth Childers Everywhere," J.J. had as volunteer workers Colum, Léon (a Russian lawyer who seems to have little to do in Paris; why, I wonder, is he cultivating J.J.? After Lucia? No, he is married) & in a less degree myself. His method is more mechanical than

ever. For the "town references," he scoured all the
capital towns in the Encyclopaedia and recorded in his
black notebook all the "punnable" names of streets,
buildings, city-founders. Copenhagen, Budapest, Oslo,
Rio I read to him.[69] Unfortunately he made the entries
in his black notebook himself and when he wanted to
use them, the reader found them illegible.[70] On the last
day he inserted punnishly the names of 60 Mayors of
Dublin (taken from the Dublin Postal directory of
1904).[71] He has been depressed lately; perhaps the
Sullivan campaign has not succeeded as well as he
hoped. I fancy he is gradually getting over his
Sullivanitis.

June 3, 1930

No, that is not so. Visiting Sylvia Beach to deliver her a
copy of my just-appearing book,[72] I hear that J.J. has
wired from Zurich asking her to reserve seats at the
Opera for a Sullivan night, for some journalists to hear
the great John Sullivan. Never have I had more things
to do and felt less inclined to do them. This "Lauriers"
preface will give trouble, I foresee; also the *Revue de
France* article. Heaven knows how Moune and I will
manage to translate bits of *Work in Progress*. No
energy. Is it the air of Paris, or a rapid decline? This
desire for rest is perhaps a kindly inspiration of Nature—but then Nature is not kind and deserves not a
capital initial.

June 23, 1930

He is back—vision slightly improved in the left eye.
Visited Dujardin with him.[73] The old man cross-
examined J.J. about dates. It seems that J.J. told
Larbaud casually about *"Les Lauriers"* in 1920. In

1922 he gave more precise reference. Valery Larbaud could not (he says) get the book—though old Dujardin says it was procurable in libraries. Meanwhile, it seems, a book of criticism appeared (by one Lalou) which *éreintait* Dujardin's work.[74] Larbaud wrote a criticism of this in *N.R.F.* without defending Dujardin. Evidently the old 'un [Dujardin] has a grievance that Valery Larbaud did not get and read the *Lauriers*. It seems that Dujardin produced a play, *Marthe et Marie,* at Geneva while J.J. was at Zurich (he was managing the English Players at the time and they were running a triple bill of three plays—all "literary"—in English, French and German[75]). J.J. wrote to Dujardin but the letter was not received. About that time Bérard gave a lecture at Zurich on the *Odyssey* which J.J. attended; but he has never met Victor Bérard. Dujardin's son was then employed at the Zurich consulate and J.J. may have met him.

Read over eighth chapter of my translation of *Lauriers* to Joyce. He approves. It seems that Sullivan's arrangement to sing at Covent Garden has fallen through, but Joyce is less cut up than one would expect. He thinks that Sullivan has an impossible character (quarrelsome and anti-Semite) and this puts him in wrong with directors. A condonation of comparative failure.

August 11, 1930

Impressions of Zermatt. Matterhorn (of course, the beginning) looks like a Sphinx, viewed by itself. Seen from the Eastern slopes of the Visp valley, like the horn of a rhinoceros, the back being the long lumpy black and white ridge which joins its base up with the

Breithorn and Zwillinge (Castor and Pollux). At six
every evening the one main street is full of Germans
mostly returning from their *Ausflugs*. Fantastic clothes.
Huge, nailed boots. Plus fours halfway down the calf.
Black puttees. Bursting brown rucksacks. Faces red and
peeling. A town of red roses. Specialities—gingerbread
embossed with the Matterhorn, children selling *edel-
weiss*, three *Seiler's* cages of "marmottes" in pairs; they
prefer dandelion leaves but eat sugar or pink sweets
with pleasure. Everything here is *Seiler*. The
marmottes' cage had an inscription *SEILERS;* might be
the German name for the beasts.[76] Little brown huts
everywhere for storing hay. Propped on mushrooms—a
large flat stone on a tree-trunk. Roofs of stone slabs.
Red walls, roofs rusty red stones and grey. Large rocks
dotted about the meadows, fallen from cliffs above.
Sound of water everywhere, the Visp (very fast, foamy,
milky, waves leaping up from the rocks in the bed) and
hundreds of irrigation channels along the slopes. To
water his field the peasant jams a slab of stone across
the runnel, which overflows. He does about a yard at a
time, meanwhile standing rigid, like a square-cut
dummy. Inscription in Gornergrat railway carriages:
"Please do not spit about." One and a half hours up
and up. Flowers get smaller and smaller as one ascends.
Bright too—vivid reds and blues. Flowering moss.
Patches of dirty snow near the top. Cliffs reddish.
Gornergrat hotel like a castle; here, as everywhere,
waitress includes 10% tip in the price demanded and
forgets to mention "service included." View from the
hotel—snow mountains on all sides. *Wunderschön.*
Many paths in hillsides round Zermatt with green seats
marked *Kurverein.*

September 8, 1930

At Lucerne. The first fortnight spent at a *pension* (Roseneck) in the Töpferstrasse behind the Schweizerhof. A leggy (bare-legged) fair Swiss married to a chauffeur brought in the morning coffee. A wild woman, wearing scanty garments that seemed always to be falling off her—showing much arm and underarm and chemise. They sleep in the next room; a child, Lina, that whines to greet the sun. In the other room adjoining mine, a musician and his girl—he tall, dark Balkan looking; she plump, dark and Didoish. He returns each night at two or three, bangs doors. She talks in a baby nasal voice, bleats Na-a-a, Na-a-a, Na-a-a. *Mach! doch nicht Schweinereien.* After lunch they make a similar noise. She is like an animal, seldom has much to say, always protesting—the female animal resisting, pretense of shame. Why not? Appetizing. But that baby voice, *viol de mineure* voice, is trying. And especially to an *hépatiquement insuffisant*, who gets a headache and feels tired as if he'd been on a three day *bombe*, if he has a mere pair of martinis or eats an ounce too much! There is a sound of revelry each night from the Schweizerhof garden which my window overlooks. The Blue Danube always enthusiastically applauded. In the corner of my room a huge stove— white-tiled; it must be seven feet high and about four feet each way. Similar one in Moune's room below. Why make them so enormous? Mystery. The house kitten disappeared; eaten, it is said, by Italians. At Lucerne cats have to be kept shut up as Christmas approaches.

Here at the Terrasse Hotel now. All notices in English on walls. Many middle-class English; an American family. Entertainment by a conjuror accompanied by "La belle Fatima" and "La fée lumière" (the same person), a blond lean woman with two chins and an aquiline nose. Second part of the entertainment—exhibition of mesmerism—catalepsy. The lady, apparently holding onto a staff, is gradually raised till she is at right angles to it; obviously jacked up, one can hear the clicks (the top of the iron staff evidently fits into a slot in some mechanical apparatus, an iron corset perhaps). As the man lowers her, he has to lift her up a little each time to free the ratchet. Next luminous dances, à la Loie Fuller. The German proprietress exclaims, "Wunderschön!"

Unable to do any useful work—feeling washed out, no ideas, no energy. Why? Something détraqué inside, no doubt. Fortnightly appeared without my article "James Joyce's New Work"—have they turned it down? J.J. insists on my adding to the Lauriers preface: (a) an account of his meeting with Dujardin. Lazare lève-toi! (b) why Moore refused to write the preface.[77] Wants me to explain that he personally doesn't give a damn about the monologue intérieur. (No more do I.) To show his superiority. The adoration of the Magi (Dujardin), the old man reverently kissing the divine child. Moore dragged in to show "controversy" about monologue intérieur, that it is a debated technique and interests literary men—but He is above such vain disputes. It is simply so much material for his talent, to be exploited, then discarded. I begin to sympathize a bit with M. Brousson.[78] It is a sad fate to be a parasite, incapable of acting for oneself—to have ideas, but not constructive ones; to be able to express oneself, but with nothing to express. Dried up, in fact. And, as soon as I try to see living people moving and acting and to write it down, a fog comes over them. When I try to hear them talk, they grow silent, and I have no words to put in their mouths. Wave of cotton-wool over the sea-bed of thought; they are a physical sensation those waves, not a metaphor. As soon as I "concentrate" or introspect I can feel them beating, washing over and over the shapes of ideas I want to grasp. It began with a loss of values. Reason is pragmatic—there's no getting over that. One can only grasp things which have some sort of importance. The others don't exist. There are important things in life, I admit—but they are not ideas, abstractions. Solid things—they have value. All ideas are fiction. So I can't write fiction. I can read it therefore the book is there. Are other people's ideas, then, more real to me than my own? Supposing self-consciousness is really a product of collective life (civilization)—*they* think me, therefore I am. Alone, would one live by sensations—reflexes? Anchorites? But unless they had been primed with consciousness in youth, they'd be dumb and insentient then. And, in fact, they have "ecstasy."

October 25, 1930

Forty-seven years ago at Bentley, Essex, that event important only to three people (two are dead) took its little place. Futility, I suppose I should say—yet what is not futility? To make a noise, be famous or infamous— all these are mere panoply. The hoplite himself is the essential, the core of the effigy, that is not effigy. And one consciousness is as authentic, as complete, as any other. The most anyone can say is "I am I" and the most "eminent" can't go further than that; Napoléon, Lenin, Mussolini said it louder than most, but it was only a question of noise, a loud-speaker adapted to their voices. I have no loud-speaker to make my voice a bray (the modern orator should on each occasion, before beginning his speech, turn to the microphone and reverently adjure it: "Let us bray"), but I can say the same thing, as validly and confidently as they.

On the thirteenth the *chambre à coucher* converted into a operating theatre. Doctor and dentist extracted five dents. Narcotic—"balsoforme." The same, remembered sensation. The feeling of being lifted up, with a roaring in one's ears, while something big comes down upon one. At each breath a sort of click of a trestle—a sort of "jack" lifting one a stage higher. Everything immense, the walls like mountains, ceiling vague, open perhaps. Everything being rhythmically puffed up, breath by breath, like a pneumatic tyre. But before it bursts, unconsciousness comes (when one is dying, I suppose, one feels the burst)— and I opened my eyes, saw them there, and wondered when they were going to begin. "C'est fini." Then I realized my mouth was full of blood, lumps of it. Weakness, retching, ignominy. Must have drank many *gorgées* of blood, very indigestible, the doctor says. Laid up nearly ten days. Lungs affected—said to be effect of anaesthetic on incipient "grippe." I wonder! Still feeling weak and short of breath; decadence. Why does one go on living when the works are obviously running down?

Literary news. Have lost contact with Joyce now. He has been busy for a month now cultivating Beecham and an American millionaire, Otto Kahn, trying to get them to take up his pet.[79] I am no longer useful, as he has a permanently attached slave in Léon. On the whole, a relief.

November 14, 1930

I rarely see J.J. now. He has started working again, but it seems to go very slowly. About 8 pages (hand-written). He got me to play over to him a number of children's games (songs) in the Novello edition. His favorite is "Looby Light."[80] We had them to dinner at Prunier's a week ago. J.J. drank well and was expansive. Believes in long dresses for women: anti-feminist. "La femme c'est rien" is one of his remarks. He wanted to stay and continue drinking but Mrs. Joyce took him away. Through the kind offices of Colonel Brown, I have got to know a Persian, Prince Farid-es-Sultanat, who wishes to publish his biography.[81] A pleasant man, age about 38. All he really is interested in is his three love-affairs; in two of these, as far as I can understand, the lady died tragically. In the last one she was murdered, run over several times by her own car. He proposes as title "Am I to Blame?"! But the Persian "Queen Mother" has put a spoke in his wheel; she won't let him reveal his identity. So the background has to be vague—an Orient *imaginaire*—and the effect will be unconvincing. A pity. Anyhow, he is ill now, and seems disinclined to continue.

December 5, 1930

The collapse on the Bourse has brought down the rents and Moune is very busy flat hunting. I doubt if—unless I insist—we shall move. She is rarely satisfied and apt to forget that *le mieux est l'ennemi du bien*. It is as well, perhaps. To be tied to Paris (how I'd have loved it even six years ago!) means little to me now—the people *je m'en fous*; but I like the book sales and concerts—to which I have rarely the energy to go, *d'ailleurs*. Lack of physical force—where's it all gone to? Swilled out by drinks, perhaps—yet I don't really think so. Rest, rest, rest. To stay *en pantoufles* all day, day after day. It looks easy, but—. The horrible expeditions to "amusements"—cinema, theatre, evening parties enslave one. Drink is the sole salvation. Even so I am too slow and timid to rouse myself to entertain or try to entertain the others. They bore me and I bore them stiff. The stiffness of age, of indifference which I can't conceal, of having no opinion on anything. No soul to sell. It has worn away to almost nothing, just as I am coming round the last segment of the circle, and beginning to believe in it. It is like coming into a fortune in extremis; *richard de la dernière heure*; extreme unction and extreme wealth.

Money. Lucia Joyce last night (at the Gaillard concert, where Giorgio was singing, chorus of course) came with mama to us in the balcony: "They're all Jews downstairs!" Nothing but evil to say of Mrs. Fleischman—the Erse way of acknowledging benefits received.

December 8, 1930

Tomorrow, wind and weather permitting, I leave for London—a dreadful *corvée,* I wished I hadn't planned the trip.

On Friday a dinner chez J.J. at which, on a bottle of Swiss wine—or a little more than a bottle—J.J. managed to get blind drunk before midnight. Fell off his chair on to the floor, talked unintelligibly. McGreevy and I helped him to bed—I said good-night and held out my hand; he pressed his lips against it![82] The family still hostile to Mrs. Fleischman and Jews in general. Anyhow Mrs. F is marrying George Joyce on Wednesday (the 11th) and can snap her fingers. I foresee a swift reconciliation. Mrs. F's presents are worth to the Joyce's at least 200 pounds a year. They cannot do without her or someone like her.

December 25, 1930

The reconciliation is achieved. Despite Joyce's predilection for the family Christmas dinner under his own roof, Mrs. Joyce has had her own way and the dinner (to which we are not invited) will take place at her daughter-in-law's. But the general meeting of the Faithful will take place as usual at his place.

Returned from London on the 17th. A lot of rushing about. Met some literates or otherwise—Stephenson, late manager of the defunct Mandrake Press, a vivacious Australian who seems to have a hobby for publishing pornography.[83] He ran the London edition of *Lady Chatterley*—but has been left with many copies on his hands, because a surplus were printed and offered by his colleague (Hachette) at lower terms to the booksellers. Curiously enough, Stephenson learnt who it was, through me. I led him to [Jacob] Schwartz's "Ulysses" bookshop and it turned out that Schwartz had been offered many copies of this hornbook at 6/- by Hachette, while the ingenuous Stephenson was asking booksellers (who naturally jibbed) a pound.[84] The way of the pornographer is hard. . . . London still has that air of stuffy congestion, the people's clothes seem too tight for them, the streets are too tight for the traffic, the air for the lungs, the windows for the air, the pubs for their denizens, who are too tight for words. This want of space is due, I think, to the Londoner's utter disregard for appearances. He is completely beauty-blind; he has none of that decorative snobbishness of the Parisian. So he arranges streets, builds houses and stations just anyhow, higgledly-piggledly; the effect is homely, but, as space is scarse, rather stifling. The conversation is similar; all is about real things, people one knows, what a good sort X is but Y's a bad sport; it never breaks loose from things known to play with flying ideas. The motors smell, the streets are muddy, repairs are blatantly obvious, like patches on Dutch trousers. They're proud of it, the Londoners; all this mess around them is like their picture of a busy factory, very active, too active to tidy up.

January 6, 1931

A singularly costly and depressing Christmas. At the Joyce's Christmas Day (evening), the usual people. Léon rather drunk and maudlin, pawing Joyce (not yet drunk enough to like it) and kissing men. One of these sloppy Russian souls who with drink get sloppier still; but no doubt they make good serfs & the Irishman is accustomed to sloppiness. Whiners & blusterers, the Irish all . . . On New Year's Eve joined the Copperies at midnight: *réveillon* at the Dome. My pocket picked in the "tambour" exit: going out, I was suddenly surrounded by a gang of shouting young men, very festive; I felt a sharp tug at the back of my paper hat (I wonder now, wasn't it my coat collar); put up my hand to keep it. At that moment one of the merry band must have slipped his hand inside my coat. Neatly done, and

the victim has no chance; he is surrounded by shouting,
singing revellers, if he saw what happened and pro-
tested, he wouldn't be heard. . . . The days pass and
none is worth marking with even a grey pebble. For all
the "use" I make of my time, whether in writing or
literary manoeuvres, I might as well be doping myself
with music or the cinema. I can't see the use of going
on manufacturing nearly unsaleable goods, which even
I myself would hardly care to buy. One needs to be a
James Joyce to put it across. (By the by, Mrs. Joyce is
quite reconciled with her daughter-in-law, whose
photograph now hangs in the salon.) The dislike for
Jews (competitors in the same line of sentiment &
business) yields quickly to the rustle of dollars. A few
well-directed gifts and the Christmas Gael is fawning
on the despised semitic feet. And why not? The silliness
was the contempt or hatred, not the subsequent
reconciliation. And why not, for money? *Lucre* both
charms and soothes the Irish breast. The John Sullivan
campaign goes on. Sullivan himself is at Genoa, where
the papers are enthusiastic (it seems) about his voice. O
purblind Otto Kahn, O pillbound Beecham, that his
pearl is cast in vain before you!

January 15, 1931

The social life is closing in around us again. The
Colums came to dinner bringing with them one Arthur
Johnson, a Boston lawyer and toper.[85] It appears that
he won the heart of one of two beautiful sisters (married), heiresses. She divorced her husband by whom she
had had two daughters, to marry Johnson. The husband took it kindly and remained on good terms with
the new menage. Then the wife died—in some rather
unpleasant manner—Molly Colum, my informant,

suggests. Arthur Johnson, she says, is now in love with the daughter, aged nineteen, the spit of her mother. She was sent here to "finish" and also to be separated from her step-father, but he followed her up—she is now in the American Hospital with scarlatina—and will take her back with him to America in a week or so. He is a queerly handsome man, very restless and wrinkled, a heavy drinker; grows side-hair down to the level of his lobes, Spanish-looking. Brief whiskers. Obviously Mary Colum regards him as her property, though she professes disgust with such "vamps" as Mrs. G.;[86] it appears that her publisher is about to produce a work by a young American and asked her to look it over— evidently, if this be so, her critical power is highly rated. The boy is a friend of Mrs. G.'s. He came over to Paris recently and, though Mary Colum asked Mrs. G. to give him her address and tell him to call, he never came. The assumption is that Mrs. G. wished to keep him to herself and suppressed the message. (But there may be an "innocent" explanation; the boy may have written down nothing and been afraid to meet Mary Colum) I suppose there is a conclusion—why not call it *carrément*, a moral to be drawn from these *faits divers*. Trivial, of course, they are—yet they illustrate the divers ways people have of making each other uncomfortable. Take the man of about my own age, Arthur Johnson, who is (we suppose) in love with girl of 19. He has "it" as the Joyce's call money and could afford to escape from the social labyrinth, to take her away with him to a lonely place and learn, uninter- rupted, if they really satisfy each other. If so, *tant mieux;* otherwise, they can return to the tingle-tangle of city life. He can absorb alcohol, she can dance with nice boys, and both be happy. But that solution is too simple. Why? Because only glaring, turbulent emotions are strong enough to lift such people out of the tangle; *au fond* they crave for such complications in their love-dances; the simple figures strike them as dull and stupid. And, no doubt, they know their own business best. If the stream is shallow one can make quite a pretty little maze out of it by dropping obstacles—taboos, just impediments and so on—here and there upon its bed. If it were deep, these bric-a-brac would be engulfed, sink out of sight. That *would* be a pity. A big river is dreadfully bourgeois, even if it travels fast and deep it makes but little fuss. It seems to me that the people who preach at one (like "Rampion" in *Point Counter Point*) to live completely or integrally, or (like Nietzsche) dangerously, generally belong to the "fussy" type. One does not need a multitude of interests to feel alive, nor need one want to exercise all one's instincts as if they were a pack of hounds. It is better to put all one's eggs into a simple well-made and ample basket (or a couple of them) and keep a firm grip on the handle than to disperse them in a myriad of flimsy contraptions, a great many of which, if not all, will surely get smashed on the long, bumpy journey deathwards. But to arrive at that dark destination, the *Terminus Camarde*,[87] with one's pair of baskets containing—let's say Love (bourgeois, banal, Stopesian Married Love) on the right, and, on the *main gauche*, let's say Intellect (bright, serene, but not passive; awake to Beauty and ensuing her)—to arrive with one's basket intact at the Douane and pass beyond unmolested—for surely, Monsieur le Douanier, such good eggs as these are not listed as "contraband," no, it's all right then, *merci* Monsieur Rousseau—to pass beyond the barrier

and see . . . what's Heaven, or just the back entrance to
the same old world?. . . and then to deposit the lucky
baskets in a celestial incubator and watch the hatching
out, birds of Paradise, fluffy Cupids and Psyches,
winged dreams, to watch and wonder—will this
sentence ever end? Never, I think, I hope . . . I can see
no ending. But I will tell you, you—I've made a note of
the date—on this day 50 years, January 15th, 1981,
when I have paid my *loyer* for the terme just ended and
handed St. Peter his trimestrial *pourboire* in exchange
for the receipt.

March 1, 1931

There is no getting out of the vicious circle. It is absurd
to talk about "finding oneself," just a piece of conceit,
but "se recueillir" might mean something. In solitude,
at peace. But these exist no longer. The little recupera-
tive *entr'acte* I looked forward to has been suppressed
by illness, not mine. That is, I suppose, how people
develop "nerves," or decide to smash things up. But
after the smash—it all grows up again like a cancer.

House hunting is ever with us. Prices are more acces-
sible, but difficulties arise at every moment. . . .

To James Joyce bi-weekly I read information concerning Angels and Devils (from Aquinas; "Le Diable" by
Abbé; Waite's "Magic") and play English children's
singing games, German children's ditto, Dalcroze and
French popular songs.[88] He is obviously bored with the
whole business, but they seem to be passing through a
financial crisis and he needs the money, or thinks he
does.

March 9, 1932

A year has passed since I wrote of the supposed
financial crisis of another. Since then, my own has
come. Financial & dyspeptic. Pornic. Three disgraces—
Serge, the Beau (in filthy khaki)—a surly sodomite—&
the prize bounder George Guntsling. All for the *beaux
yeux* of that shrill singer and overpainted sister of little
Mimi. Blurred memories.[89]

Then the nightmare of moving into this flat, myself ill
and M. unwilling. Nightmare on nightmare. Next—by
way of solace—some translations: *Formes*, *Vol de Nuit*
and half *L'Innocent* taking all my little energy. Strug-
gling to do things well—and rarely succeeding . . . and
all for nothing in a world of barbarians and callow
exhibitionists. I decline to forgive them because they
know not what they do; for they pretend to know.
They are the sort who would as editors correct
Flaubert's French or James Joyce's prose, substitute
"clever like he is" for "clever as he is," who believe
that Sophocles studied Freud and Shakespeare was a
votary of the Revolution of the Word. Revolution!
Because a few amenities are left, a little culture still
remains, they want to *émeuter* the vulgar horde against
it, laboriously educate the scholars in inhumane
illiteracy, make their children into blustering whiners
and wailers like themselves. Hysteria and ill-temper
and aggressions on all who are wiser or better "cultured" (hateful word!) than themselves. And the poor
little things fancy they are persecuted; too illiterate
even for the journal-fed mob, they believe there is a
cruel conspiracy against them, that the bourgeois is
shaking in his shoes lest their Rimbaldian balderdash
should upset the applecart.

March 26, 1932

The Joyce-Sylvia Beach battle seems to have begun
last year. Joyce, at the time of his son's marriage,
wishing to have some dowry for that penniless
youth, proposed to settle ? on him a share of the
Ulysses rights. Therefore he had a contract made
with Sylvia Beach which he claims to have signed
"blind." The purport was that, in the event of the
publication of *Ulysses* in America or England, Sylvia
Beach was to have the right of fixing the royalties,
etc. and negotiating. Saving clause: she was to act
"in the interest of the author" and he was to approve of the arrangement made. She started negotia-
tions but (according to J.J.) wanted a preposterous
advance, 5000 dollars each. The need for publication
in America appeared urgent to J.J., because there
was a pirated edition being sold on a large scale (at 7
or 8 dollars), an exact facsimile of Sylvia Beach's
edition (the figures and some other details were
different). J.J. also heard that it was "down" on the
English literature course of some American university. He estimated that he could sell some 30,000
copies on the strength of this.[90] He was told that the
"pirates" had printed 8000 copies.[91]

This struggle began in November 1931 or thereabouts,
J.J. wanting Sylvia Beach to alter the contract, but
never himself definitely asking her to do so.

But, early in the new year, Adrienne Monnier had
dared (horror!) to write an aggressive letter to him.
Subject: the fee of 1000 francs from the *N.R.F.* for the
translation they published of *Anna Livia*.[92] J.J. proposed that the sum should be divided between the

translators; she pointed out how little that would mean for each. He suggested they should have a dinner on the proceeds. Her letter said that Gide had been round and spoke of Joyce's disinterestedness. She had been careful not to give him away, though (she said) she knew he was really very keen on money. He lived extravagantly, travelled first class, though she and Sylvia Beach had to travel third. (I wish I could remember the details—an amusing letter.) Also, over the telephone, Sylvia Beach had, it seems, called Joyce a liar. He and his family were very bitter, told everyone about how he had been ill-used and sent various emissaries to negotiate. The Jolas pair worked up and fervent partisans. (Clever to tell Mrs. Jolas who, as usual, retailed the news to everyone. Still it doesn't seem to have got into the papers, which was doubtless what Joyce was aiming at.)

April 26, 1932

Other partisans were the Colums. A letter or article appeared in the *New York Catholic Herald* attacking Joyce personally (the Colums refused to let me see it. Why?)[93] Result was Mrs. Colum, lukewarm formerly, developed into a champion. The emissaries sent to negotiate (Colum with Beach, Soupault with Monnier) got no definite result, though it seems that Sylvia Beach told Colum that, as J.J. thought the contract unfair, she would destroy it. Meanwhile, to replace this maid-of-all-work of his, Joyce had worked up a liaison with one Paul Léon, a Russian Jew, a lawyer. (He is still doing the secretarial work B. used to do and writing to publishers etc. for Joyce).[94] Meanwhile the air at No. 2 Avenue St. Philibert[95] was dark with lamentations of hard-upness (which didn't prevent long daily taxi drives and costly dinners at the Trianon). I went there every Thursday and Friday and heard progress of the campaign. Joyce refused any interview with Sylvia Beach. His fixed principle is—never act oneself, cultivate ostensible "aloofness" and pull strings. Then came his birthday, February 2. Mrs. Jolas volunteered to have the ceremony at her place. She did it well. A pudding (iced) made up to look like *Ulysses* with 50 candles round it, for the Jubilee. J.J. sent S.B. a present (clever move, though a little forced as it was *his* birthday)—two book supports, "biches" from Brandt's shop.

May 3, 1932

To continue. A few days later the surrender came. Miss Beach wrote to say the contract was annulled and he was free to dispose of *Ulysses*. At once he got in touch with publishers. Several offers. Finally accepted Cerf's.[96] A Jew and a friend of his daughter-in-law. Colums rather sick about it; they had found a Xtian publisher and believe that there would be a better chance of getting past the censorship if a Jew (and one who, it seems, had a name for publishing outrageous books) were not to sponsor *Ulysses*.

About a month ago J.J. was due to leave for England. He was in the train with his family when Lucia made a scene. Wouldn't leave Paris. So they all bundled out again. The luggage had to be taken out of the van. I arrived just when this had been done. The truth is none of them really wanted to go.[97] We all went to lunch at the Mariniers.

Lucia, inspected by Dr. Fontaine, was ordered 12 days' rest in bed instead of the smacking she rightly deserves.[98] The three stayed at Hotel Belmont. Mrs. Joyce looked for a flat, but half-heartedly, as her son (who now esteems himself a financier) told her to wait. A dreadful crash coming, according to him. Joyce, of course, declined to take any meals at his hotel. So evening after evening they dined out and Joyce became half seas over. Mrs. Joyce, who is nearly as jumpy as her daughter, got more and more *énervée*, blaming him for everything—that they have no home, that the girl was ill and so forth. Unjustly, as I think—for she is just as fretful and capricious. The truth is that all their lives (even his) are empty. They do not attach themselves to anything except ephemeral things, and tire of these so soon they are always at a loss. Thus they never, or rarely, make friends. Too self-centred. J. himself is the most human (doubtless his wife was quite human once but she caught his attitude and, as women do, pushed it too far); but he, too, cannot settle down to continuous work or make friends for friendship's sake. Hence the Sullivan campaign, the anti-Beach campaign. To fill his life he pictures himself as a victim pursued by enemies, and will not understand that most people are indifferent—e.g. "le cas Sullivan"—neither for, nor against. Other people's troubles or joys leave him cold; he is never interested in the "human" side of a book or tale or event. Hardly even the literary. It's just a fact to him. Unless it concerns his family (father, for instance) or, in a less degree, his country. Nationalities interest him a little. He has still the naive enthusiasm—a little of it—for self-proclaimed rebels and the naive belief that people who have morals are hypocrites.

On Thursday at 12.45 J.J. arrived looking very red. I was just starting my solitary lunch. He has taken two places at the Comédie Française; there is some wonderful actor (I forget his name) playing in a short play—*Le Châtiment*. I volunteer to join him at 2.20. (It is Ascension Day.) Then he explains that his wife is threatening to leave him. She has said she will no longer stand him "tumbling about" each night. He believes (or persuades himself—and me, too!) that it is serious this time. We meet at the theatre. He is fascinated by the play—cries bravo! enthusiastically at the end. (Incidentally wishes his wife were with him; the play has an Italian setting.) Outside the theatre, he becomes anxious again, wonders if she has gone really. We walk part of the way to his hotel. Then he takes a taxi. He gets to telephone from a *bistrot* near the hotel. Reply: "Mrs. Joyce left five minutes ago." We proceed to the hotel. The bedroom is as usual. Her slippers beside the bed. I take him to tea at Berry's. Return to hotel about 6.15. Porter informs him she is there. He goes up by himself. I remain in reading room. After a quarter of an hour porter asks me to go up. Mrs. Joyce is by herself. Tells me it's all over, she won't live with him any more. (Joyce thinks that, when she took his pocket-book to pay the restaurant the night before, she kept the change on 1000 francs.) She seems determined. Locks up her boxes; I help. She does not weep but looks very red and gives little snorts from time to time. J. returns, curls up in a chair in an attitude of dejection. Says he can't arrange for himself, must have her. Suggests they go away together for a change. She tells him she wishes he would drown himself. Says he gives her and Lucia an unbearable life, is responsible for everything. Then goes and sits on an armchair looking out the window. Talks of the money he has wasted on Sullivan and on tips; that is why they can't afford to have a decent flat now. Joyce has just received some 20,000 francs (advance from America on *Ulysses*). Offers to pay a year in advance. She insists on going, says she will pass the hat round to her friends. Then I have to go; dining chez Kahane at 7.30. Joyce asks me to ring him up. (I tell him I'm at his disposal on Friday.) At 7.45 I ring up. Mrs. Joyce answers, says she's "given in again." So that's that.

May 24, 1932

The interest has centred for the last 20 days round Lucia. The typical girl left to herself and developing in all her selfishness. It is absurd to say that she never had a chance; she had every chance. Only her conceit and idleness prevented her from trying for either of the things she wanted—becoming another Pavlova or making a good match. She cultivates her father's imperious airs and spells of silence. And few young men in these times of free and facile conjugation would put up with that. Illiterate in three languages, professing the feminist desire to "work" and having the feminine aversion for any work that is not directly exhibitionist or concerned with embellishing her body—"work," as she sees it, meaning a well-warmed and elegant office where she, the Worker, shines like a jewel before the admiring gaze of employer (if any) and employees, respectful, subservient and prompt to spare her every last *démarche*—, utterly deficient in "it," yet expecting every man (young and old)—woman, too (nowadays why not?)—to do his duty in amusing her, feeding her, supplying her with dresses, she has at last run up against realities. No, not quite. In the Colums, to whom add Mrs. Harmsworth, she finds people to fawn over her.[99] [Padraic] Colum like a little dog wagging his tail at her. (Yesterday Joyce rang Colum up on the 'phone, beginning with his usual gruff "Well"—the tone of a pitiless commander questioning some abject subaltern on the results of a mission.) There have been so many *péripéties* that it's hard to set the facts in order. A week or so ago—say May 17— Lucia was suffering from insomnia, or professed to be, and decided she could never sleep in the St. Philibert flat. So she moved down to Léon's—a small flat, packed with people. They are a servile lot and should have suited her well. Joyce and Mrs. Joyce, however, persisted in seeing her there. Their prejudices against Jews had infected Lucia and, though her fiancé is an intimate friend of George Joyce, the latter's wife dissuades his sister from the marriage—the repugnance of the rich Jew toward the poor and well-bred one. For Alexander Poniatowski [sic] belongs to the Jewish "aristocracy" in Russia and has got a Cambridge degree; he speaks English with hardly any accent.[100] All this is irritating to a German Jewess of the New York slums. Then, too, like his sister, Madame Léon, he is dignified in manner; that incenses his prospective *beaux-parents*. J.J. has a monopoly in that line and hates competition. "Silence, exile and cunning" are his specialty, for (as he knows) silence is the most telling sort of exhibitionism and "exile" in France the supreme luxury for a writer; the land where they say "cher maître" to any *littérateur* whatsoever. J.J. himself is in a predicament, however. In Léon he has an ideal secretary, replacing Miss Beach. Also how about Mme. X? Three weeks ago we dined [with] the Joyces at Reine Pédauque. Towards the close—when he was *en train de* "partir"—J.J. grew sentimental. "Norah [*sic*], you've been a good wife to me." "I won't see that woman again." She intervened abruptly: "Shut up! You're talking nonsense." Moune heard this—she may have *mal entendu*—but, if she's right, Mme. X seems indicated. Those are the only persons he sees; it couldn't be anyone else.[101]

After four or five days Lucia found the Casimir-Perrier flat [Léon's] insupportable and moved to the Colums' (ex-Jolas flat, Rue de Sévigné). They welcomed her enthusiastically. Colum is a philanderer and his wife was glad to entertain Joyce's daughter. She had proposed to take Lucia over to Dublin with her. (The first visit for 20 years of a member of the Joyce family would doubtless be quite an event in local literary circles.) Lucia professed great nervousness. Insisted on Mrs. Colum sleeping in the same bed with her. While still with the Joyce's she had made her mother sleep in the room with her. Her father asked her why. She merely said, "La finestra!" Neat. The man Alex came frequently to see her there. The Colum's didn't take to him. Too dignified for them, I expect. She came to lunch here and was quite cheerful and normal; realized, I suppose, that we are not impressed by hysterics. Young Ponisovsky [*sic*] came after lunch and took her for a walk.

July 9, 1932

She stayed with the Colums about ten days. Meanwhile she worried the maid by her curious questions. "Have you had a lover? Do you think every girl should marry?" (This sort of question strikes the amateur psychologist as rather insane. To me it seems merely

Joycean: the expression of whatever comes into one's head without the least shyness, indifferent to what people may think {except for a certain joy in shocking them}. That is a way of attracting attention and hence a favorite device with Lucia and her father).

The Colums, simple souls, played up to her, listened to what she said, never left her alone. Molly C. had to sleep in the same bed with Lucia. The young fiancé (for it appears that there was a *dîner de fiançailles* chez Léon where he and Joyce got royally drunk—What kisses! What Russian squirms!—) came to see her and Lucia proposed to cook his dinner for him. (This is, it seems, one of Lucia's ways of showing affection. Mrs. Joyce, wishing to prove to me that Lucia was at one time really in love with Beckett, explained to me that when they were away from Paris Lucia had asked him round to the flat and cooked dinner for him. Judging by Lucia's general incompetence, I should say this meal was rather a test than a proof of love. Anyhow, Beckett seems to have dropped Lucia pretty quickly after that; a beefsteak *alla* [*sic*] Lucia may have been too much for him.

All was going well, the dinner in process of being cooked, when Lucia came to the Colums and announced that she and her boy had decided to dine out instead. The Colums had a fixed idea—perhaps orders from Him—that she must not go out with Ponitowsky [*sic*]. Dramatic scene. Colum stood before the door like Horatio but the limber maid eluded him and dashed down the stairs and out into the street, where it was raining. There he pleaded with her—hatless, sans umbrella, invoking pneumonia and his deep compunction. To which she yielded, queenily compassionate. But when they reached the *quatrième* the little lover had volatized. None saw his exit; he had not left by the street door. The Colums think he ascended to a higher story and lurked *in excelsis* till the storm had passed. But I suspect a menial exit—*l'escalier de service*.

While chez les Colum, Lucia renewed her parrot-cry: "I want work." Then unluckily for her she addressed it to Mrs. Harmsworth with whom one day she lunched. This simple lady took her at her word. Old Dr. Howard, the entomologist of the Quai d'Orleans, was for the moment without his secretary. Mrs. Harmsworth arranged for Lucia to go there next morning. Dr. Howard dictated some letters to her; then (as she claimed to know German) he asked her to translate a German letter. The attempt failed, of course. When Lucia came back to lunch that day she showed signs of exasperation. The Colums were furious with Mrs. Harmsworth. Fancy trying to make the poor girl work like that! Mrs. Colum tried to get Moune and me to interview Mrs. Harmsworth, with a view to cancelling an engagement for lunch with her which Lucia had made. Naturally we declined. So Mrs. Colum took steps, and Lucia was saved from that *mauvaise frequéntation*. The Howard episode was ended.

Meanwhile a nerve specialist, Codet, had been called in to see Lucia. His visit was fixed for the day, as it happened, when Lucia was lunching with Mrs. Harmsworth. He arrived at the Colums at 2. Lucia was still away. The Colums had decided (the suggestion was doubtless Joycean) that Lucia must not know she was being diagnosed. So Mrs. Colum had an inspiration; she phoned to Lucia explaining that a French doctor had come to see her (Mrs. Colum) and would Lucia return to interpret as she could not understand him. Thus the doctor had to examine Lucia via Mrs. Colum. The latter, however, left the room for a time on a pretext, so the doctor had a few minutes alone with Lucia, and could converse with her and justify his opinion that she needed a rest cure—or surveillance—at one of the establishments mentioned by him. Costly places, of course; J.J.'s eagerness to overpay is touching and those who have something to sell him graciously respond to it. It is delightful indeed to feel one is giving and receiving pleasure by the same act.

July 20, 1932

Why do I go on writing about these people? *Au fond,* they interest me so little; a few bright moments when they are comic is the most to expect—like an American funny film. Here the comedy is certainly subtler than usual, for it seems that Lucia, by playing her part so well, has come to be dominated by it and is, in some respects, genuinely out of her wits. Probably, *au fond,* everyone is insane and sanity (as we call it) is instilled into us by the teachers of self-restraint and proper sentiments. Once we repudiate these there is no knowing how far we shall go—murder, melancholia, suicide, all are possible. After all, one's first emotion, when a desire is denied, is to mope or curse or break things. What restrains us? *Bon sens,* you say—but is *bon sens* ever inborn? And then the greatest desire is, with many people, to be in the limelight. That can be attained by making scenes. If you feel neglected, scream or break something; that will make them sit up and take notice. Presently the screaming and breakage become enjoyable in themselves, even without an audience. That is insanity.

The doctor, it seems, advised complete seclusion for another six weeks or so, but J.J. (why I wonder?) refused to consent. Instead of that he fixed up a trip for her, accompanied by her nurse, to Feldkirch in the Tyrol where the Jolas family is summering.

July 28, 1932

Another Lucia incident I remember. Just before leaving for Austria Lucia spent a day and night at an hotel in Passy. There an elaborate comedy was played by Joyce (who asked me to come with him). From the concierge's office he had that lady telephone to the nurse that she was wanted at the telephone. When she came down Joyce handed her a sum equal to her railway fare. As soon as we were upstairs and in Lucia's presence, the nurse ostentatiously handed her railway fare to Joyce, who asked her for it. (He had told the nurse to mix up the money in her bag—he had given her an odd sum, say 357 francs—to make sure the payment had an impromptu air.) The theory is that the nurse is travelling with Lucia at her own expense! She wanted a holiday and decided to spend it with Lucia's welcome companionship! When Joyce saw Lucia a week or so before, he said to her: "I propose that you pay half the nurse's expenses and will give you the money for it." Lucia replied: "Let her pay for herself."

August 6, 1932

Had Kahane and his Armenian friend, Manoukian, to dinner last night (an expensive meal, completely ruined by the incompetence of the maid). Kahane is a queer type; his character is a blend of avarice, amorism and snobbery, but the result is not unpleasing. In his passion for "banned" books there is something more than self-interest; yet he is not D. H. Lawrence. He believes in love-making (love-mucking?) as man's proper study. The proper-improper. Thus just now he professes enthusiasm for the book *Storm* by Peter Neagoe (Jolas's friend); I am sure that if the U.S. Customs had not excluded it, he would have esteemed it dull.[102]

He has a great readiness to get *emballé* for any woman who appears smart to him, and he claims that he is unable to write novels unless he is in the throes of a love-affair. That is typical, I think, of the occidental author. Art is often a by-product of passion. Subject for an essay. Wagner, Dante . . . *Autrefois,* the religious emotion, too. Much "unrest" of the times is due to sexual dissatisfaction, I imagine. The inborn and ineluctable craving for romance in conflict with the will to almost mechanical conjugation, and the spirit which bids a man talk of his "mate" rather than his wife (the bestial, *Urwelt* pose). Two beasts mating in the modern jungle, peopled by bus-mastodons and aero-pterodactyls. The chained forces of prehistory (coal, petrol, electricity) released and recreating the lost primitive world. What am I doing in this galley? Dying out, I suppose. Frankenstein and Gertrude Stein. The only thing would be to be rich enough to keep out of the current. But they take care that backwaters shall be above the means of such as I. And the only way to earn the price of one is to go down into the *mêlée.* And even if I tried to do that, they wouldn't have me.

If I could write of peace! Or romance! There are
thousands waiting for a book that will promise them
escape from these conditions. I know what is wanted—
but the energy or imagination fails me.

August 15, 1932

Naïvetés I've written! "Thousands waiting for a book."
Must have read it in a blurb: "This is the book that
thousands have been waiting for." No one is waiting
for anything much except his daily bread, beer and
block. Those are the targets. And I, too, turn in much
the same circle, except that I'm too restrained or worn
out to bother much about the third item of the trinity.

Romance—perhaps a fiction of the ecstatic amorist.
The reconciling of sex with religious idealism; the
elevation of the holy organ. *Sehnen nach Liebestod.*
Those who have will to live reject it. But then, perhaps,
life isn't worth living. There's no way out. In love with
death, in death with love.

The "charming" people, Padraic Colum for instance,
have diverted the stream into two channels, philander-
ing and literature. All the hormones nicely bisected:
fissioned caviar.

August 19, 1932

After dinner joined Maria Jolas and her mother at
Ledoyen's where they'd dined. The old lady
(Mrs. Macdonald) is as bright as the average woman of
half her age. Rather like Mrs. Crosby senior, but
perhaps less *mondaine,* more spontaneous. Yet in the
plain common sense and energy of these ladies one sees
the germ of the new *Américaines*—dogmatic, callous,

egotistic. They have, for instance, the typical modern
mania for travel. Men are sweating in America and
their machines are ruining the economies of the
civilized countries just in order that these noisy and
ignorant women may dash from Edinburgh to
Salzburg, to Cannes, Paris and Copenhagen, and play
the little autocrat wherever they go, finding simple
refinement "so quaint" and human dignity and [the]
odd museum piece. They come and see and conquer;
even Frenchwomen are infected by their restlessness—
their empty heads and hearts. It is easier to empty a
head than to fill it. Epitaph for a great Irishman: I
came, I saw, I whimpered.

November 5, 1932

Of personal history these last months, little. A month
excursion ticket (second class, of course, and—pro-
vided it's not too numerous—the company in second is
more congenial) to La Bretagne. Halts—short at
Quimperlé and Quimper, long at Benodet. In one's
fiftieth year, the state of health is a preoccupation, and
I offer here a white phagocyte to Eugenia, thanking her
kindly for her recent *gentillesse*. . . . The financial
shadow is heavy this autumn, and of course the High
Command has now decided that this unlucky flat (in
which I had hoped we both would take joy and pride)
must now be furnished willy nilly. Why? It's like telling
a dying man to buy a new outfit of clothes. No use
whining, however.

J.J. seems undisturbed by the fall of the £ and the
depression. He has sold *Ulysses* rights to the Albatross
and they have given a fat advance. I suspect, too, that
his investments were shifted into dollars in time, or has

he found another Maecenas?[103] The neurotic Lucia
seems to have quite recovered and is interested, above
all, in her publicity. She has, I think, some talent, and if
she worked for the glory of God, not her own, would
make a little name in the world of missals, evangelaries
and the like. And that is, perhaps, what she will do.
Meanwhile, however, there seems to be a conspiracy
on foot to send her back to "observation," i.e. a half
madhouse. Her charming sister-in-law is in the movement, also the woman doctor Fontaine. The Jolases,
always on the scent of neuroses, hallucination and the
like, adorers—like all good Americans—of the medi-
cine-man, concur. Set a thief to catch a thief is under-
statement; set a thief to trap an honest man is no less
true, and people who themselves are "touched" are
quickest to see insanity in others. I wonder if the
heretic-hunters in the past were not themselves half-
sceptics. There is nothing Freudian in it; simply the
prescription of an ideal just beyond one's reach, to spur
oneself on towards perfection. The wholly honest man
takes his honesty for granted; the potential thief
preaches honesty in order to reform himself.

January 1, 1933

There is no way out of the circle of desires and failures.
The cloud of unknowing hides all the exits, or: the
exit—for there is, most likely, only one for each man.
For a while one thinks that money is the one thing
lacking; but now I know it can help very little indeed,
except to buy a spell of forgetfulness from time to time.
There is nowhere to go. Only a fool appreciates the
praise of fools—that is success. Yet, I suppose, that
kind of folly, given the success, is the ideal solution.
Money, celebrity, personal charm—these would justify

men as we find them, and our social lives. Otherwise the stone rolls back upon us every time and the labour is more obviously vain than if one had succeeded in pushing it to the top and watched it rolling freely down the further slope.

January 3, 1934

A diary which contained one entry for each year should, I suppose, be called an annuary. That would make a title for a book: "Mrs. Winter's Annuary." The brave new formula might win success; the lady's soul-states and husbands year by year; the gradual process of her ethereal soul towards nirvana, where not one man but all men, indeed all living things, are her mates, and the whole universe is a chunk of dope, succulent, somniferous and satisfying. That, and no less, would, I imagine, meet the modern woman's omnivoracity—but why did I write "modern woman," when the feminine in this world of bloody flux is the one constant and only man's attitude to her has changed?

About myself—for, after all, these yellow pages were intended for an obscene purpose—what of that year 1933? It was eventful as the one year since 1907 when I have spent more than a casual month or two in England, the only year in which I damaged myself seriously in an accident.

Every man of sense and fifty [years of age] has always been a *laudator temporis acti;* optimism (or, rather, hopefulness) is so constant in the young that their idea that (largely thanks to their efforts) the world will be a more agreeable place to live in than it was for their parents, is natural enough. And they have faith in progress and inventions; toys. . . . It is and always has been obvious that England is going to the dogs, or—shall I say?—bitches. What is happening is a levelling down and up, a tuning in of the average mind to broadcast and other "dope," and a willingness to accept as pleasure whatever is held up to the public as pleasurable in newspapers etc. And, of course, freedom, irresponsibility.

Meanwhile our fortunes have been steadily declining thanks to the efforts of the gangster-president of U.S.A. The little I can make by translations is inadequate. *Formes* has collapsed. From September last, for five months, I have toiled away at "Les Thibault"—a hundred pounds or so.[104] And a hundred pounds today only represents about sixty real pounds, enough to live on for five or six weeks. But that is what my work is at the utmost worth; I have no illusions about it—except (and that isn't an illusion, I believe) that I am better than most of the younger generation of translators and the Americans—which isn't saying much. And since the English papers and, I suppose, the doped population have come to regard President Stavisky of the U.S.S.R. (the allusions will be lost or anyhow stale in a year or two[105]) as a paragon of Presidents, very likely Messrs. Lane will refuse to pay me—on economic grounds, or postpone payment till there has been a free deal round of depreciated pounds by a progressive government. Of course it is great fun for very young people and for those who have little to lose. It also satisfies the peevish middle-aged, represented by Aldington and company, who believe that Victorian hypocrisy set up a barrier between them and the girls on whom they wished and failed to work off their desires. They talk of a chastity complex—but mayn't it simply have been that the girls in question were—discriminating? A handsome and agreeable man will not have to trouble much about the chastity of his girls—or only to wish that they had more of it and would pester him less. The famous modern "revolt against morality" is, I imagine, the work of ugly duckings.

March 26, 1934

The past year still remains unaccounted for; or isn't its empty space best passed over in silence? I am not interested in my soul—no one except a Xtian (or other "believer") need be interested in it. We went to a play last night, *La Joueuse*, where a sex-ridden woman prated a lot about her soul. Her soul—well I never heard it called that before; still the "âme" might be decoded into "con," and "soul" to "cunt." "Âme," for instance, is solved by the formula 2.2.9.—but I can't justify the number; a job for cryptogrammatists.[106] That is the curious thing—materialists so soon become immaterial, and, though they exploit the good old words like "soul" and "decency" and "honest," really neither believe in them or understand them. *À force de* believing in behaviourism, the Americans are really becoming automata, controlled by reflexes only, "conditioned" as they say. Words have become mere pejorative or approving noises, or signals for action. That is where I sympathize with Jolas in his "Revolution of the Word."

On February 6th we went "en ville" to see the *émeutes*. I should have gone alone or with a man. On such occasions a woman, particularly a headstrong woman, is a needless complication; she is alternately too prudent and too rash and, worst of all, won't obey orders. But, I suppose, obeying orders on a *soir d'émeute* is almost bad form. *Liberté, Egalité, Froternité* (the "o" in honour of the famous M. Frot, the minister who made himself so unpopular by letting the police fire that night). We reached the Opéra without difficulty; people standing about, a few mounted police and "agents," but no excitement. We went into the little bar adjoining the Café de la Paix in front of the Opéra. For a quarter of an hour—*le temps de boire un café-crème*—nothing happened. Then a rush of people went past the door. The little "bar" has no shutters, large plate glass windows. The proprietor put out the lights. At the back of the café is a long aquarium, along the wall, lit from behind. The fish showed up in the darkness—fat, sedate creatures, staring with goggle eyes and open mouths at the excitement of the "proprio" and some of the customers. And yet one can hardly admire their *sang-froid,* for they would be the first victims of an incursion. A crowd thronging against the tank or a stray bullet would abridge their golden superiority and leave them gasping and curvetting on the floor. Lack of imagination, that's all. A dog, more imaginative, would have been impressed, quivering with excitement. . . . The noise in the street declined, the lights went on again. We moved cautiously along the right pavement of the Boulevard des Capucines toward the Madeleine. Two processions passed, carrying banners with patriotic inscriptions, one singing the *Marseillaise,* the other shouting "Dé-miss-ion!", meaning they wished the Chautemps cabinet to resign—as it did the next day.[107] The Place de l'Opéra had, however, been declared a "zone neutre," and of course the procession made a point of passing it instead of taking by-streets. When the second procession came near the "place," a number of police, *gardes mobiles,* rushed out of side streets and tried to disperse them. There was a rush back along the boulevard and the *gardes mobiles* began to lay about them with revolver butts. No shots were fired. We retreated into Viel's restaurant. Several wounded men were brought in; the waiter who saw them knocked on the head was indignant. He said they were inoffensive spectators. Still, on such occasions, spectators are obviously a nuisance, and really less entitled to consideration than the "manifestants." On the whole a futile demonstration; the demonstrators other than the Royalists had no definite purpose, except to make the then government resign. They had merely been worked up by papers into an hysteria of honesty, outraged by Stavisky & co.

Stuart Gilbert on James Joyce, Herbert Gorman, and Paul Léon

Stuart Gilbert, probably Paris, 1936–1938, at work on the English titles for Sacha Guitry's film, Les Perles de la Couronne *(1936). See note 67.* HRHRC Collections.

Have just read, skipping the lumps of pudding, Gorman's book on Joyce.[108] It was bound to be a failure for, clever as Joyce was, his pride prevented him from letting his biographer put in the little details and anecdotes that would have shown the real Joyce—a great man with a little mind; highly sensitive and quite ruthless; a natural intriguer, born litigant, slave-driver, and on occasion, the most charming companion; so self-centered that he took no interest in others except in their relations to himself or as possible material for the artist. Adolf Hitler and he had much in common, I should say. His charm was always calculated, his generosity intended to impress—when it was not an appeal for reciprocity. Thus resumed, it sounds [like] an ugly character; yet one could see Joyce for what he was, and still like him. As one likes a cat, not asking from him the qualities of a dog; there was much in him of the feminine.

Gorman unfortunately was no Boswell. And even Bozzy would have turned out a dullish book, I suspect, had Johnson insisted on each page being vetted by him and all the foibles sublimated. For since self-worship is natural to man, Joyce's self adoration made him very human in that respect. He only carried to a high degree what we all feel about ourselves. Still, had he known he was to die before the book appeared, he would have given his biographer a freer hand most likely. He was clever enough to know that the man himself was far most interesting than the lay figure

Gorman built up under his orders. A whole chapter would have been given to the description and illustration of the method by which he got people to put their time—and sometimes money—completely at his disposal; to follow him wherever he wanted them to accompany him: boring plays and operas, dull expensive restaurants; to [cancel] their engagements if he wanted their assistance in some trivial, easily postponed task; to run errands for him, pull strings for him, undertake delicate and distasteful missions which exposed them to snubs, rebuffs, and ridicules at his bidding.

For instance during the last ten years he nearly always had his letters written by one of his followers; he seldom wrote or signed a letter. He liked to have his publishers, friends, benefactors and even relatives receive letters beginning: "Mr Joyce asked me to let you know, etc.", and signed by some person who was obviously not a secretary or amanuensis, but an admirer. (It is quite understandable that he would not reply in person or sign letters to his "fans" who in many cases were mere autograph hunters. He wished to keep [up] the market price of Joyce [autographs]. I remember him showing me a bookseller catalogue of autograph letters and his satisfaction in seeing one of his priced higher than a letter signed by Edouard VII.) Gorman perpetuated the legend that Paul Léon was unpaid. Not that Léon would not have worked "for love"—quite literally for love. His devotion to Joyce was dog-like; he had the manner of a large, fussy, affectionate collie dog. There was much warmheartedness in that worthy Russian, whom Joyce was careful to describe, whenever opportunity arose, as a man of high intelligence, and vast knowledge. He may have had knowledge but he gave the impression of being half-witted and I am convinced the Léon savoir-faire was another Joycean fiction, a matter of prestige. Léon's wife [was] a hard, shrewd but attractive woman, certainly . . . as such, and she ought to know. If, as I think, Joyce paid Léon, he did so partly out of generosity, and partly to conciliate Léon's wife, who had to work for her living as a dress-maker's agent, with a mainly American clientele, I believe.

Selected Letters from James Joyce to Stuart Gilbert

Portrait of James Joyce, with an inscription to Gilbert, dated January 16, 1932. HRHRC Collections.

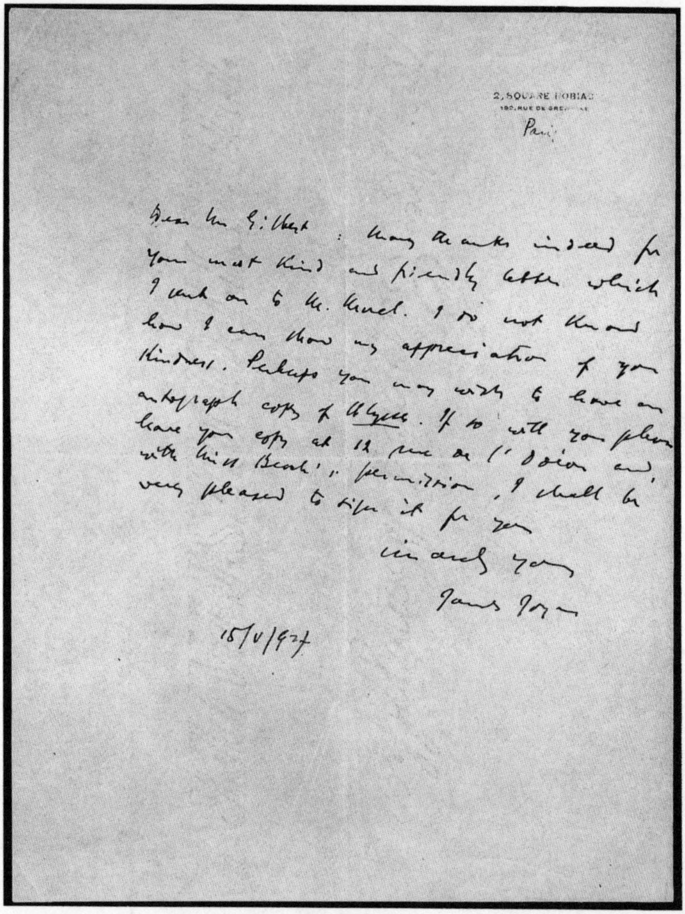

Letter from Joyce to Gilbert, May 18, 1927. HRHRC Collections.

Autograph letter signed
[May 18, 1927]

2 Square Robiac, 192 rue de Grenelle, Paris

Dear Mr. Gilbert:
    Many thanks indeed for your most kind and friendly letter
which I sent on to Mr. Morel.[109] I do not know how I can show
my appreciation of your kindness. Perhaps you may wish to
have an autograph copy of *Ulysses*. If so will you please leave
your copy at 12 rue de l'Odéon and, with Miss Beach's permission, I shall be very pleased to sign it for you.

Sincerely yours,

James Joyce

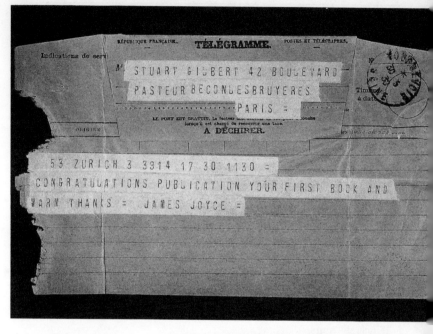

Telegram from Joyce to Gilbert, postmark June 30, 1930. HRHRC Collections.

Telegram
[Postmark June 30, 1930
Zurich]

Congratulations publication your first book and warm thanks.[110]

James Joyce

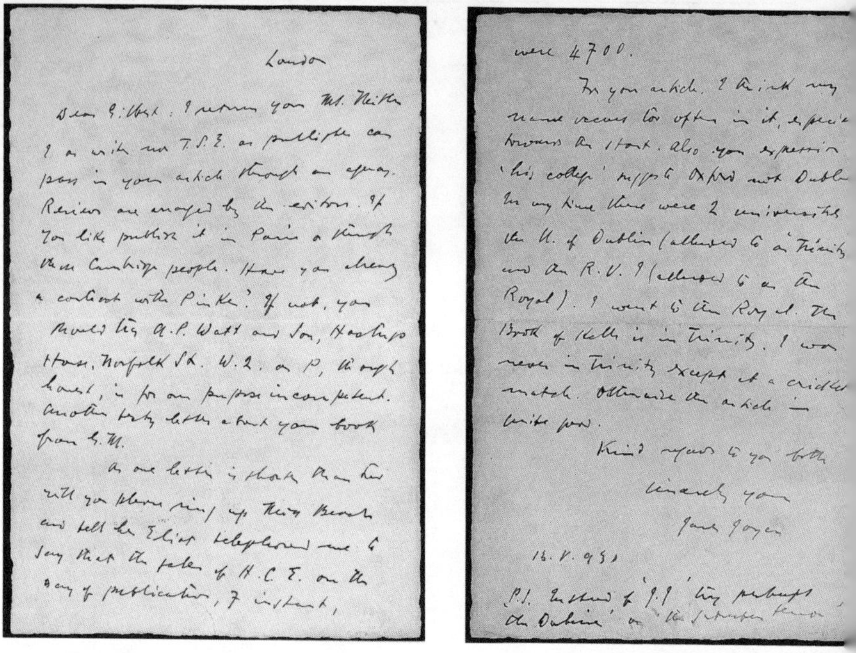

Letter from Joyce to Gilbert, May 13, 1931. HRHRC Collections.

Autograph letter signed
[May 13, 1931]
London

Dear Gilbert:

I return your ms. Neither I as writer nor T.S.E. as
publisher can pass in your article through an agency.[111] Reviews
are arranged by the editors. If you like publish it in Paris or
through those Cambridge people. Have you already a contract
with Pinker? If not you should try A. P. Watt and Son, Hastings
House, Norfolk St. W.2 as Pinker, though honest, is for our
purpose incompetent. Another testy letter about your book from
G.M.[112]

As one letter is shorter than two will you please ring up
Miss Beach and tell her Eliot telephoned me to say that the sales
of H.C.E. on the day of publication, 7 instant [?], were 4700.

For your article, I think my name occurs too often in it,
especially toward the start. Also, your expression "his college"
suggests Oxford not Dublin. In my time there were two universi-
ties—the U. of Dublin (alluded to as "Trinity") and R.U.
(alluded to as the Royal). I went to the Royal. The Book of Kells
is in Trinity. I was never in Trinity except at a cricket match.
Otherwise the article is quite good.

Kind regards to you both,

Sincerely yours

James Joyce

P.S. Instead of "J.J" try perhaps "the Dubliner" or "the
suburban tenor."

ce 5 mars 1932

Dear Gilbert,

Please send the Correspondant article in
an enveloppe to Miss Harriet Weaver,Castle Park,
Frodsham,near Warrington,for I am sending you by
this post an integral copy of the review for Harm..
worth which he should send when read to Duff
explaining to him what a Gough he has made concernin
my effect on catholic readers.

J. J.

P.S. Say nothing about
the Ulyses affair for
a few days

Letter from Joyce to Gilbert, March 5, 1932. HRHRC Collections.

Typed letter initialed with autograph postscript
[March 5, 1932]

Dear Gilbert,

     Please send the *Correspondant* article in an enveloppe [*sic*]
to Miss Harriet Weaver, Castle Park, Frodsham, near
Warrington, for I am sending you by this post an integral copy
of the review for Harmsworth which he should send when read
to Duff explaining to him what a Gough [*sic*] he has made
concerning my effect on catholic [*sic*] readers.[113]

J.J.

P.S. Say nothing about this *Ulysses* affair for a few days.[114]

HOTEL MÉTROPOLE
NICE
FRANCE
17·10·932

Letter from Joyce to Gilbert, October 17, 1932. HRHRC Collections.

Autograph letter signed
[October 17, 1932]

Hotel Métropole, Nice

Dear Gilbert:

I cannot ask Léon to attend to this as it is about Lucia. I want 12 copies of *Paris-Midi* (4 Octobre) and 2 copies of *Courrier des Arts* —money under separate cover. Useless for you to go to a newsagent. The best way is to go direct to their office. I have just heard that the Dover Customs have seized and sequestered the 10 copies of Lucia's book sent (and almost all sold) in England on the ground that they are "silk goods" (the casing is silk) and are asking a high luxury tax. Kahane and Harmsworth should have foreseen this step of their fellow-countrymen.[115]

Can you thank Jolas on Tuesday by 'phone for his letter to me? Tell him also I was informed last night by those who ought to know that we are not returning to Paris but remaining here. His interpretation of Jung's letter is not mine. If Jung wanted to be humble he could have been so in this public article. I am glad I kept him at a distance. It seems as if he needed some first aid himself.[116]

I am trying to work.

Sincerely yours,

James Joyce

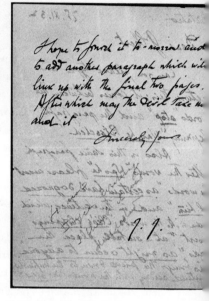

*Letter from Joyce to Gilbert, November 25, 1932. HRHRC
Collections.*

Autograph letter dictated, perhaps initialed by Joyce
[November 25, 1932]

Dear Gilbert,

    Can you please type and return this; it comes between the words *"stop"* and the paragraph beginning *"Was he Pitsseled."*

    Also in this same paragraph after the words *"Was he"* please insert the words *"as certain have dognosed of him"* and in the sentence which ends with the words *"Clio's clippings"* insert at a suitable place the words *"as might occur to anyone."* This brings the piece down to the unfinished sentence ending with the words *"Our river."* I hope to finish it to-morrow and to add another paragraph which will link up with the final two pages. After which may the devil take me and it.[117]

Sincerely yours,

J.J.

Postcard from James and Nora Joyce to Stuart and Moune Gilbert,
August 26, 1936. HRHRC Collections.

Autograph postcard signed
August 26, 1936
[Elsinore, Denmark]

Greetings from here.[118]

James Joyce
N. Joyce

Notes

1. The importance of this collection, with its significant revelations and extensive research material, will be discussed more fully in *Joyce Studies Annual* 5 (1994).

2. An epithet for Helen Fleischman, Joyce's daughter-in-law, that was based on her father's profession: Adolf Kastor made his fortune as a cutlery manufacturer in New York.

3. André Germain (b. 1881), French literary critic and historian; social acquaintance of Caresse and Harry Crosby (see note 53). Robert McAlmon (1896–1956) expatriate American writer, founder of Contact Publishing Company, and friend of Joyce's (Richard Ellmann, *James Joyce: New and Revised Edition* [New York, NY: Oxford University Press, 1983], 514. Referred to hereafter as "Ellmann").

4. John Rodker (1894–1955), English translator, poet, and publisher of the Ovid Press. He published the confiscated Egoist Press edition of *Ulysses* (October 1922) and contributed an essay, as did Gilbert, to *Our Exagmination round His Factification for Incamination of Work in Progress* (1929). His archive, as well as that of his press, is at the Harry Ransom Humanities Research Center.

5. Helen Nutting; she and her husband, Myron C. Nutting (b. 1890), an American painter, lived in Paris from 1919 to 1929 and were longtime friends of the Joyces.

6. In 1917 Joyce had composed a parody of this song entitled "Dooleysprudence" (Ellmann, 423–425).

7. Marie Monnier, sister of Adrienne Monnier and wife of Paul Bécat, was an artist and weaver. In 1928, she made for Joyce a "wonderful carpet . . . representing the [Liffey] flowing through Dublin into the Irish Sea with the arms of Norway; Dublin; Ireland and my own all woven into the scheme" (Ellmann, 606). In 1930–31 Joyce asked her to prepare a pictorial or "hieroglyph" preface for the "Children's Games" section of *Finnegans Wake* which Jack Kahane proposed to publish in a deluxe edition under the title *Chapelle d'Izzied*. See *Letters of James Joyce* III, ed. Richard Ellmann (New York, NY: The Viking Press, 1966), 209, referred to hereafter as *Letters III*. Due to difficulties with Faber and Faber, personal problems in the Joyce family, and the rupture with rue de l'Odéon over *Ulysses*, nothing came of the plan. The passage was finally published in *transition* 22 in 1933 and in deluxe booklet form in 1934, under the new title *The Mime of Mick, Nick and the Maggies*, with an initial letter and tailpiece illustrations by Lucia Joyce.

8. "A" probably refers to Stuart Gilbert's wife, Moune. He marked the "A" with red in the diary manuscript for a future correction that was never made.

9. Victor Bérard (1864–1931), French translator and critic of the *Odyssey*, author of *Les Phéniciens et l'Odyssée* (1902–1903).

10. The de Velnas are unidentified. William Aspenwall Bradley (1878–1939), American writer, translator, editor, and literary agent in Paris, was married to Jenny Serruys (b. 1886), translator of *Exiles*. The extensive Bradley archive is at the Harry Ransom Humanities Research Center.

11. Stuart Gilbert kept notebooks on his talks with Joyce, both for his own work and for Joyce's future reference. Some notebooks contained extracts from books Joyce wanted to use or read for his work. These notebooks are part of the Gilbert collection at the Harry Ransom Humanities Research Center.

12. *Victor, or Children in Power* (1928) by Robert Vitrac (b. 1901).

13. For Ford Madox Ford's written account, see *It Was the Nightingale* (1934), 270–271.

14. *La Tragédie de Salomé* (1907) by the French composer Florent Schmitt (1870–1958). Olga Spesivtseva or Spessiva danced with the Marlinsky and Diaghilev ballets.

15. Nora Joyce re-entered the clinic at Neuilly for a hysterectomy operation on February 5, 1929. See Brenda Maddox, *Nora: The Real Life of Molly Bloom* (Boston: Houghton, Mifflin, 1988), 246–247, referred to hereafter as *Nora*.

16. The proofs were for the third watch of Shaun (*FW* 474–554) which appeared in *transition* 15 (February 1929). See *The James Joyce Archive*, ed. Michael Groden, et al. (New York and London: Garland Publishing Company, 1978–), 59:1–51, referred to hereafter as *JJA*.

17. This was not the case for long. By the time *transition* 16/17 (June 1929) came out, Gilbert had been made a contributing editor and had taken over some of the work of answering critics, reading manuscripts, making translations, and proofreading. See Dougald MacMillan, *transition 1927–1938: The History of a Literary Era* (New York, NY: G. Braziller, 1975), 60.

18. Ernst Robert Curtius (1886–1956), German scholar and author of *James Joyce und sein Ulysses* (1929) and articles on Joyce (*Neue Schweizer Rundschau*, Heft 1 [January 1929]).

19. Gilbert refers to his own work, *James Joyce's "Ulysses"* (London: Faber and Faber, 1930).

20. Desmond MacCarthy (1877–1952), prolific English literary critic. Sisley Huddleston (1883–1952), newspaper correspondent and author of many books about France.

21. *Ulysse, traduit de l'anglais par m. Auguste Morel, assisté par m. Stuart Gilbert* (Paris: La Maison des Amis des Livres, 1929).

22. Among the Joyce circle Monnier and Beach were jokingly known as "Scylla and Charybdis" because their bookstores were on opposite sides of the rue de l'Odéon.

23. The final contract, dated April 4, 1929, gave Joyce $2000. The fragments were published by Harry and Caresse Crosby and appeared under the title *Tales Told of Shem and Shaun* (Paris: The Black Sun Press, 1929).

24. A reference to Léon-Paul Fargue (1878–1947), French poet and acquaintance of Joyce, who assisted with Jacques Benoist-Méchin's translation of passages from *Ulysses* into French. Joyce encouraged Fargue to translate *Anna Livia Plurabelle*, though nothing came of the plan.

25. Cyril Connolly's "The Position of Joyce" appeared in *Life and Letters* 2, no. 2 (April 1929): 273–290. Gilbert's concern was unfounded as the article contained no mention of his discovery of a connection between the endings of "Nausicaa" and *A.L.P.*

26. Probably Adrien Copperie, French poet, author of *Cirque* (Gallimard, 1936). Copperie and Gilbert translated poems of Caresse Crosby which appeared in *Cahiers GLM* 4 (1937).

27. Francis de Miomandre (b. 1880), whose article, "Vulgarisation," appeared in *Les Nouvelles Litteraires* (April 6, 1929). Gilbert's article, *"L'Ulysse de Joyce,"* appeared in *La Nouvelle Revue Française* (April 1, 1929): 567–579.

28. German playwright Hermann Sudermann (1857–1928).

29. This typescript, after some revision by Joyce, was used in setting up the first proofs of *Tales Told of Shem and Shaun*. It is now at the Beinecke Library of Yale University (see *JJA* 47:193–200; 53:97–119; 57:339–352).

30. Emile Fernandez (1900–1971) was a friend of George Joyce with whom Lucia Joyce was "briefly in love" (Ellmann, 512). He was the brother of Yva Fernandez, French translator of *Dubliners* (1926), which was one of the earliest translations of Joyce's work. See David Hayman, "Shadow of His Mind: The Papers of Lucia Joyce," *The Library Chronicle of The University of Texas at Austin* n.s. 20/21 (1972): 65–79. See also David Hayman and Ira Nadel, "Joyce and the Family of Emile and Yva Fernandez: Solving a Minor Mystery," *James Joyce Quarterly* 25, no. 1 (1987): 49–57.

31. Chapters from Gilbert's study, *James Joyce's "Ulysses."*

32. Joyce was "complicating" matters with last minute revisions of the proofs that kept the Crosbys in "a state of controlled fury" (Ellmann, 614).

33. Lewis Melville Irby, an English teacher who compiled indices for Gilbert's books, was a friend of Gilbert's since Oxford. (Letter from Gilbert to Peter du Sautoy, 13 March 1951, Harry Ransom Humanities Research Center.)

34. Gilbert's article, "An Irish Ulysses—The Hades Episode," appeared in *Fortnightly Review* (1 July 1929): 46–58.

35. "Revolution of the Word Proclamation," *transition* no. 16/17 (June 1929): 47. The manifesto was signed by Kay Boyle, Whit

Burnett, Hart Crane, Caresse and Harry Crosby, Martha Foley, Stuart Gilbert, A. L. Gillespie, Leigh Hoffman, Eugene Jolas, Elliot Paul, Douglas Rigby, Theo Rutra, Robert Sage, Harold J. Saleson, and Laurence Vail.

36. According to Moune Gilbert, the Adnets were not literary people. Monsieur Adnet had worked at the Galeries Lafayette before launching his own business selling *de luxe* furniture. Stuart Gilbert met him when buying furniture and their acquaintance was not long.

37. Gilbert's "Joyce Thesaurus Minusculus" appeared in *transition* 16/17 (June 1929): 15 *et seq.*

38. This expression is a variation on the motto of Dublin: "The obedience of the citizen is the felicity of the town" (cf. *FW* 140.06).

39. Jesting.

40. Aldershot was a World War I military training center southwest of London. A tattoo consists of outdoor military exercises with music.

41. While in Torquay, Joyce was helping Gilbert complete his book, listening to each chapter and making preparations for publication. Yet by 1937 Joyce's appreciation of Gilbert's work had diminished. Upon being asked by Vladimir Nabokov about the Gilbert collaboration, Joyce replied, "A terrible mistake, an advertisement for the book. I regret it very much" (Ellmann, 616).

42. "Mr. James Joyce," *Spectator* (3 August 1929): 162.

43. "Mrs. S." is perhaps Daisy Sykes, Claude Sykes's wife. After Torquay the Joyce entourage visited the Sykeses at Letchworth.

44. Robert Bridges (1844–1930) sent a copy of his book, *The Testament of Beauty* (Oxford: Clarendon Press, 1929), to Joyce with the inscription, "To Mr. James Joyce from the author in hermeneutic sympathy, R.B. Oct. 1929."

45. In his research for *Finnegans Wake*, and especially during this holiday, Joyce purchased a selection of trade journals and popular periodicals, including: *The Baker & Confectioner; Boy's Cinema; The British Baker; Fur and Feathers, Rabbits & Rabbitkeeping; The Furniture Record; The Furnisher and the Hire Trade Review; The Hairdressers' Weekly Journal; Justice of the Peace and Local Government Review; The Modern Boy; Municipal Journal and Public Works Engineer; The Optician and Scientific Instrument Maker; Poppy's Paper; The Post Magazine and Insurance Moni-*

tor; School-Days; The Schoolgirl's Own; The Thriller; The Tri-umph; Woman; and *Woman's Friend*. Most of these were saved and are now at the University of Buffalo; see Thomas E. Connolly, *The Personal Library of James Joyce* (Buffalo: University of Buffalo, 1955), 56–57.

46. In 1930 Faber and Faber published Gilbert's study, *James Joyce's "Ulysses,"* as well as Joyce's *Anna Livia Plurabelle*.

47. John McCormack (1884–1945), an Irish tenor who was especially popular in America in the 1910s, and with Joyce through the 1920s (*Letters III*, 32).

48. *The Morning Post* (19 December 1929).

49. In a letter of June 7, 1924, to Louis Gillet, Edmund Gosse described Joyce as "a literary charlatan of the extremest order." The complete letter is reproduced in Louis Gillet, *Claybook for James Joyce* (London and New York: Abelard-Schuman, 1958), 31–32.

50. Probably the book dealer Jacob Schwartz. "The bearded image of J[esus] C[hrist]" may refer to Schwartz having been the model for a painting of Christ, perhaps by the English painter Stanley Spenser, though this is speculative.

51. Factorovitch, whose first name was perhaps Stuart, assisted Joyce as a secretary in 1929 and was referred to by Joyce as his "foreign-born admirer."

52. Edward Titus (1870–1962), American bibliophile and *littérateur* living in Paris, was owner of the Sign of the Black Manikin press and bookstore, and editor of *This Quarter* from 1929 to 1933. On February 28, 1927, Titus bought the final corrected page proofs of *Ulysses*, which are now housed at the Harry Ransom Humanities Research Center.

53. Harry Crosby (1898–1929) was a wealthy American expatriate, publisher and poet. With his wife, Caresse Crosby (1892–1970), he founded the Black Sun Press. On December 12, 1929, he shot Josephine Rotch, the "Mad Queen" of his love poetry, and committed suicide. See Geoffrey Wolfe's *Black Sun: The Brief Transit and Violent Eclipse of Harry Crosby* (New York, NY: Random House, 1976).

54. Presumably for *47 Letters from Marcel Proust to Walter Berry* (Paris: The Black Sun Press, 1930).

55. The Black Sun Press published *Alice in Wonderland* in 1930 with Marie Laurencin's illustrations. Laurencin (1885–1956) had given art lessons to Lucia Joyce.

56. The final year of Harry Crosby's diaries was published posthumously as the *Third Series* in 1930 by the Black Sun Press.

57. When William Bird suggested that Lucia's squint should be corrected, Joyce replied that "some people find it attractive" (Ellmann, 611).

58. Probably *Haveth Childers Everywhere* (Paris: Henry Babou and Jack Kahane, 1930). The edition of *Anna Livia Plurabelle* that Gilbert refers to, though not a *de luxe* edition, is probably the Faber and Faber edition of 1930.

59. According to Danis Rose, the presently confirmed number of city-entries in the *Encyclopaedia Britannica* (11th edition) plundered for notes amounts to 41 and filled the best part of two notebooks (both of which are now at the University of Buffalo). In order of inscription, these are: (i.) Belfast, Lisbon, New York, Mecca, Warsaw, Madrid, Vienna, Christiania, Bucharest, Cairo, Budapest, Berlin, Athens, Brussels, Copenhagen, Amsterdam, Constantinople, Peking, Prague, and Sofia (all from *JJA* VI.B.24); (ii.) from notebook VI.B.29: Stockholm, Tokyo, St. Petersburg, Delhi, Bern, Belgrade, Buenos Aires, Edinburgh, Mexico City, Ottawa, Kabul, Melbourne, Washington, Wellington, Teheran, Rangoon, Dublin, Rio de Janeiro, Paris, London, and Bristol. In addition, *JJA* VI.B.29 contains brief references to Fez and Tunis, but, apart from "Kasba," these do not seem to have inspired any puns. For an earlier version of this list see Danis Rose and John O'Hanlon, *Understanding "Finnegans Wake"* (New York, NY: Garland Publishing, 1982), 339–340. See also Ellmann, 628.

60. Helen Fleischman.

61. Count Gerald Edward O'Kelly de Gallagh (1890–1968), educated at Clongowes Wood College, in 1929 became the first Irish Minister to France. He retired in 1935 and, remaining in France, started a wine business.

62. Jack Kahane, publisher of Obelisk Books, and Henry Babou, a Paris publisher of *de luxe* editions; together they published 600 *de luxe* copies of *Haveth Childers Everywhere* in 1930. The costly

venture brought them close to financial ruin until the remaining copies were bought by Elbridge Adams, owner of the Fountain Press in New York. See Jack Kahane, *Memoirs of a Booklegger* (London: M. Joseph, 1939).

63. Giacomo Lauri-Volpi (1892–1979), Italian tenor, sang Rossini's *Guillaume Tell* at La Scala in 1929.

64. "Prote: Ulysse" appeared in *Echanges* (March 1930), 118–134. "Harry Crosby: A Personal Note" and "Astropolis" were published in *transition* no. 19–20 (June 1930). The essay on Robert Bridges never appeared in *transition*. Schwab is unidentified, though he may have been a film composer.

65. Nicholas Nabokov (1903–1978), composer, cousin of the novelist.

66. Wife of Adrien Copperie. See note 26.

67. Kervin and Schwab are unidentified. Gilbert was involved in various film projects in Paris, including writing a "Sketch of a Scenario of Anna Livia Plurabelle," which Joyce encouraged him to do, later making "a number of suggestions for its improvement." See *A James Joyce Yearbook,* ed. Maria Jolas (Paris: Transition Press, 1949), 10–19. Gilbert here proceeds to describe a film shooting he attended; unfortunately the film and Gilbert's exact role are unidentified. Later, in 1936, Gilbert wrote the English subtitles for Sacha Guitry's *Les Perles de la Couronne* (Pearls of the Crown), an extravagant French trilingual history of the pearls of the English crown—from Henry VIII through the twentieth century.

68. Actually, Joyce was urged to see Professor Alfred Vogt in Zurich by two Swiss admirers, Georges Borach and Marthe Fleischmann, who had learned of Joyce's ailment through an article in *Neue Zuricher*. Professor Vogt was also recommended by two other Zurich residents: the architectural historian, Siegfried Giedion, and his wife, art-critic Carola Giedion-Welcker (Ellmann, 622).

69. See note 59.

70. Some of this notebook is nearly illegible. See *JJA* VI.B.29.

71. The names of the Lord Mayors of Dublin chosen by Joyce appear on the first four pages of notebook VI.B.28 in the *JJA* and are listed in Danis Rose's preface to the notebook, *JJA* 35:xviii–xx.

72. Joyce sent Gilbert a telegram from Zurich, postmarked June 30, 1930: "Congratulations publication your first book and warm thanks." It is reproduced elsewhere in this volume.

73. For further background on the relationship between Joyce and Dujardin, see Thomas F. Staley, "James Joyce and One of His Ghosts: Edouard Dujardin," *Renascence* 35, no. 2 (Winter 1983): 85–95. Gilbert translated Dujardin's *Les Lauriers sont coupés* (Paris: Librairie de la Revue Independante, 1888) as *We'll to the Woods No More* (New York, NY: New Directions, 1938).

74. René Lalou (1889–1960), French literary critic, wrote several reviews of Joyce's work. See items 216, 1892, and 1944 in Robert H. Demmings' *A Bibliography of Joyce Studies*, 2nd edition (Boston: G.K. Hall, 1977).

75. Felice Cavollotti's *Il Cantico dei Cantici*; Danville's *Le Baiser*; Browning's *In a Balcony*. The performance took place on 11 December 1918.

76. Seiler is probably a family name.

77. See article by Thomas F. Staley, "The Irish Exile in Paris: James Joyce and George Moore," in *"Ulysses": Cinquante ans après* (Paris: Didier, 1974), 15–23. See also, Adrian Frazier, "Rapprochement with a Very Old Man: Joyce's London Meetings with George Moore," *Joyce Studies Annual* 3 (1992): 228–236.

78. J.-J. Brousson, secretary to the novelist Anatole France, wrote a "tell-all" book about his employer.

79. Sir Thomas Beecham (1879–1961), English orchestra conductor; Otto Kahn (1867–1934), German-born New York banker and patron of the arts.

80. "Looby Light," a "circle game," appeared in the children's songbooks of the English firm, Novello and Company (1912). Participants dance while singing, "Here we dance the looby, looby, Here we dance the looby light, Here we dance the looby, looby, on a summer's night." Shortly before enlisting Gilbert's talents, and before incorporating the song into the draft referred to above (where it appears as "And they leap so looply, looply, as they link to light. And they look so loovely, loovelit, all in nuptious night"), Joyce had noted down "looby light" in *JJA* VI.B.32, p. 181 (see *JJA*: 36: 404, and *JJA*: 51: 21).

81. Colonel Brown was a retired British Army officer settled in a Paris suburb. Prince Farid-es-Sultanat, a distant relative of the Shah of Iran, divorced in 1936 an American, Doris Mercer Kresge, former wife of the retail king Sebastian S. Kresge.

82. Thomas McGreevy assisted Joyce with his work, wrote an essay for *Our Exagmination . . .*, and later became director of the National Gallery of Ireland.

83. P. R. Stephenson (1901–1965) founded the Mandrake Press in London with bookseller Edward Goldston in 1929; the press was defunct by late 1930.

84. Hachette, a major book distributor.

85. Arthur Johnson (1881–1936), a Boston attorney.

86. Most likely Herbert Gorman's first wife, Jean, or second wife, Claire.

87. A *camard* is a snub-nosed person; the feminine form, used metaphorically, means *death*.

88. Many of the notes deriving from this reading appear in *JJA* VI.B.33. Émile Jaques-Dalcroze (1865–1950), French composer, was founder of the eurythmic system of musical training through physical movement. One of the many courses Lucia Joyce had taken for dance was the Cours Jaques-Dalcroze (Ellmann, 612).

89. Pornic is a seaside resort in Brittany which Gilbert might have visited. The other references, deleted in the typescript version of the journal, remain unidentified.

90. Joyce was pleased to write Harriet Shaw Weaver on October 27, 1931, that New York University was teaching *Ulysses* (*Letters* III, 232–233).

91. For an account that disputes the illegitimacy of Samuel Roth's "pirated" edition, see Adelaide Kugel's "Wroth Wrackt Joyce: Samuel Roth and the Not Quite Unauthorized Edition of *Ulysses*," *Joyce Studies Annual* 3 (1992): 242–248.

92. Monnier wrote this letter on 19 May 1931 (Ellmann, 664). The French translation of *Anna Livia Plurabelle* appeared in *La Nouvelle Revue Française* 19, no. 212 (1 May 1931): 633–646. The translators were Samuel Beckett, Alfred Peron, Ivan Goll, Eugene Jolas, Paul Léon, Adrienne Monnier, and Philippe Soupault.

93. *Catholic World* CXXXII (March 1931): 641–652.

94. "B." is Sylvia Beach.

95. Joyce's address from 14 October 1931 to June 1932.

96. Bennett Cerf, publisher at Random House.

97. This story is also told in an unpublished letter to Harriet Weaver dictated by Joyce and typed by Gilbert (British Library Add MS 57351 fols. 40–42), dated April 17, 1932, the day of the *contretemps* at the Gare du Nord.

98. Dr. Thérèse Fontaine had been Nora Joyce's gynecologist since 1928. Brenda Maddox described her as "beautiful, a feminist and a member of a distinguished family" (*Nora,* 324). Dr. Fontaine prescribed bedrest and the medication Veronal for Lucia, who had been in a near catatonic condition since the dissolution of her engagement to Alex Ponisovsky (*Nora,* 376–377).

99. The wife of Desmond Harmsworth, English painter.

100. Alexander M. Ponisovsky, brother-in-law of Paul Léon, had a degree in economics from Cambridge University. Ponisovsky introduced Joyce to Paul Léon in 1928, at which time Joyce was taking lessons in Russian from him. The Nazis arrested him in April 1944, and like Léon, he disappeared in a prison camp. See Mary and Padraic Colum, *Our Friend James Joyce* (Garden City, NY: Doubleday, 1958).

101. In the original manuscript of Gilbert's journal the identifying initial of Mme. X has been excised with a blade. There is speculation that the Gilberts mistook a joke between J. and Nora concerning Joyce's imaginary liaisons for a more serious infraction.

102. Peter Neagoe's . . . *Storm; a book of short-stories, with an introductory letter by Eugene Jolas* (Paris: New Review Publications, 1932).

103. Gilbert's assumption was wrong; Joyce was very upset, and his investments had not been converted. In an unpublished letter of October 29, 1932, to Harriet Weaver he wrote, "Now to my horror I find the £ has dropped to 82 francs 90 and is expected to go on tumbling." Stuart Gilbert collection, Harry Ransom Humanities Research Center.

104. Roger Martin du Gard's *The Thibaults*, translated from the French by Stuart Gilbert (London: J. Lane, 1939).

105. The Stavisky affair was a French financial scandal of 1933 that sparked considerable public unrest. Alexandre Stavisky, a financier,

was found dead on January 8, 1934, shortly after the bonds of his credit organization in Bayonne were proved worthless.

106. The formula 2.2.9 signifies the number of letters between "a" and "c," "m" and "o," and "e" and "n," changing the French word *âme* (soul) into the English word *con*.

107. Camille Chautemps (1885–1963), French politician who served three times as premier of France, in 1934 resigned the premiership after accusations of complicity in the Stavisky affair.

108. Dated March 1941, this untitled fragment was written upon Gilbert's reading Herbert Gorman's *James Joyce: A Definitive Biography* (London: The Bodley Head, 1941). A carbon typescript is located in the Gilbert archive.

109. Joyce refers to Gilbert's letter of May 9, 1927, written upon his seeing several pages of typescript from the translation of *Ulysses* by August Morel and Valery Larbaud. Gilbert was soon deeply involved in the translation.

110. Joyce refers to Gilbert's *James Joyce's "Ulysses."*

111. T. S. Eliot at Faber and Faber. The article in question is Gilbert's "The Joycean Protagonist," *Echanges,* no. 5 (December 1931): 154–157.

112. Probably George Moore. For more information about the relationship between Moore and Joyce, see note 77.

113. Joyce refers here to Charles Duff, *James Joyce and the Plain Reader* (London: Desmond Harmsworth, 1932), 25, in which Duff suggests that Catholic readers need disinfection after reading Joyce's work.

114. See March 26, 1932, entry in Gilbert's journal.

115. The initial letters for Joyce's *Pomes Penyeach* (Paris: The Obelisk Press, 1932) were designed by Lucia. Twenty-five copies of the book were printed in France (plus an unspecified number of copies *hors commerce*) and bound in green watered silk.

116. See Ellmann, 659.

117. On page 254 of *Finnegans Wake* one can see the fate of these changes in the final text: "Was he Pitsseled" became "Was he pitssched" and is not preceded by "stop" (which appears at 252.31); "as certain have dognosed of him" remained intact, though it does not

appear after "Was he," but after "for an ensemple"; "as might occur to anyone" does not appear in the sentence which contains "Clio's clippings"; "our river" is nowhere to be found as the paragraph ends instead in a "gulch of tears."

118. While Joyce was in Denmark he was reading the proofs for the first British edition of *Ulysses* (London: John Lane, the Bodley Head, 1936) (Ellmann, 693).

Index

Factorovitch, [Stuart?], 16–17,
90n.51
Fargue, Léon-Paul, 7, 87n.24
Farid-es-Sultanat, Prince, 34,
94n.81
Fernandez, Emile, 9, 88n.30
Fernandez, Yva, 88n.30
Finnegans Wake, ix, 3, 5, 7–8,
13–14, 18–19, 21–22, 26–27,
43, 81, 86n.7, 87n.16,
87n.23, 87n.24, 88n.29,
89n.45, 90n.46, 96n.117. *See
also Anna Livia Plurabelle;
Haveth Childers Everywhere;
Work in Progress*
Fleischman, Helen, 3—7, 13,
16, 20, 35-36, 85n.2
Fontaine, Dr. Thérèse, 46, 58,
95n.98
Ford, Ford Madox, 4
Formes, 42, 60
Fortnightly Review, 10, 31

Germain, André, 3, 85n.3
Gide, André, 17, 44
Gilbert, Moune, x, 14, 24, 34,
42, 52
Gilbert, Stuart: archive of, ix,
xi–xiii; assists composition of
Finnegans Wake, 21–22, 26–
27, 41, 81, 86n.11; bio-
graphical background on,
ix–xiii, 32; criticizes Irish,
37–38, 57; criticizes "proletariat," 14; and French
translation of *Ulysses*, ix; and
Herbert Gorman, 67–68; on
Joyce's personality, 46, 67–
68; on life in Paris, 35; on
London, 36–37; at Lucerne,
30–32; makes "Thesaurus" of

Joyce words, 10; meets Joyce,
x; proofreads "Ondt," 13;
temporarily loses contact
with Joyce, 33; thanked by
Joyce for book, 73; writes
film scenario for *Finnegans
Wake*, 92n.67; at Zermatt,
28–29
Gorman, Herbert, 67–68,
96n.108
Gorman, Mrs. Herbert [?], 39,
94n.86
Gosse, Sir Edmund, 15, 90n.49
Guitry, Sacha, 65, 92n.67
Guntsling, George, 42

Hachette (book distributor), 36,
94n.84
Harmsworth, Desmond, 77, 79
Harmsworth, Mrs. Desmond,
4, 52
Haveth Childers Everywhere,
20, 26, 75, 91n.58
Howard, Dr. [?], 52
Huddleston, Sisley, 6, 16,
87n.20

Innocent, L', 42
Irby, Lewis Melville, 10, 12,
88n.33
Ireland, 7, 13, 27, 37, 50

Jaques-Dalcroze, Émile, 41,
94n.88
*James Joyce's "Ulysses": A
Study*, ix, 5, 9, 14, 67, 73,
87n.19, 89n.41, 90n.46,
96n.110
Jazz, 9
Johnson, Arthur, 38–39,
94n.85

Jolas, Eugene, 3, 10, 15–17, 19, 44, 54, 58, 61, 79
Jolas, Maria, 18, 44–45, 54, 56, 58
Joueuse, La, 61
Joyce, George (Giorgio) (J's son), 7, 15, 25, 36, 88n.30
Joyce, James: "battle" with Sylvia Beach, 43–46; Christmas, 1930, 37–38; converses with Gilbert during drive, 7; correspondence of, 70–83; as dancer, 16–17; described by Jolas, 19; and daughter, 19, 53–54; dramatics of, 13; and Dujardin, 27–28, 31; first contacts Gilbert, x, 71; and French translation of *Ulysses*, 6; generosity of, 53; and George Moore, 31; and Gilbert's work on *Ulysses*, 8–10, 89n.41; and John Sullivan, 15, 18–19, 20, 21, 23, 26–28, 33, 38, 46, 48; and Jung, 79; with Marcel Proust, 5; misunderstandings with Nora, 47–50; on Mozart, 9; notebooks of, 4, 86n.11, 91n.59; personality assessed by Gilbert, 46; pleased by popularity of *Ulysses*, 43; prose style of, 42; reaction to the depression, 57–58, 95n.103; relates anecdote about Ezra Pound, 5; and songs, 3, 34, 41, 93n.80; suggests nicknames for himself, 75; at Torquay, 12–14, 89n.41; and wine, 35–36; in Zurich to see oculist, 26. *See also Finnegans Wake; Ulysses*
Joyce, Lucia (J's daughter): at concert, 35; dance lessons for, 94n.88; erratic behavior of, 46–54, 95n.98; eye problems, 19, 20; as illustrator, 58, 79, 86n.7, 91n.55, 96n.115; at party, 3; romantic life of, 26, 88n.30, 95n.98; "wouldn't leave Paris," 45
Joyce, Nora (J's wife): desire to go to Ireland, 13; difficulties with husband, 16, 46–48; health of, 5–6, 87n.15; "reconciled with daughter-in-law," 38; sends postcard from Denmark, 83; on social occasions, 3–4, 12, 16, 34, 36
Joyce, Stanislaus (J's brother), xii
Jung, Carl, 79

Kahane, Jack, 22, 48, 54–55, 79, 86n.7, 91n.62
Kahn, Otto, 33, 38, 93n.79
Kastor, Adolf, 85n.2

Lady Chatterley's Lover, 36
Lalou, René, 93n.74
Larbaud, Valery, x, 27, 96n.109
Laurencin, Marie, 20, 91n.55
Lauriers sont coupés, Les, 27–28, 31, 93n.73
Lawrence, D. H., 55
Léon, Mrs. Paul (Lucie), 68
Léon, Paul, 26, 34, 37, 44, 48, 68, 79, 95n.100
Life and Letters, 8
London, 36–37